Emerging Careers: New Occupations For the Year 2000 and Beyond

Volume I

The Newest of the New

by   E   70

S. Norman Feingold

and

Norma Reno Miller

About the authors . . .

Dr. S. Norman Feingold is President of the National Career and Counseling Services in Washington, D.C. For many years, he served as National Director of the B'nai B'rith Career and Counseling Services. He holds the bachelor's degree from Indiana University, the master's from Clark University, and the doctor's from Boston University. He has served on the national boards of most of the major associations in the guidance field including a term as President of the American Personnel and Guidance Association. He has written over 45 books, hundreds of articles, and is a frequent speaker and consultant in the guidance field. For years, he has had a special interest in the future and its impact upon occupational opportunities.

Norma Reno Miller has an extensive background in career information, combining a career in public relations with development of occupational abstracts for such fields as accounting, coal mining, horticulture, and building construction. For many years, she wrote and edited newsletters, annual reports, and other special publications for clients. She holds the bachelor's and master's degrees from the University of Wisconsin. Professionally, she has written on both communications (authoring *Influencing Others Through Persuasive Speaking*) and guidance (co-authoring with Dr. Feingold, *Your Future: A Guide for the Handicapped Teenager*).

ISBN 0-912048-32-8
LC 83-080074

Copyright © 1983 S. Norman Feingold and Norma Reno Miller

Published and distributed by the
    Garrett Park Press
    Garrett Park, Maryland 20896

TABLE OF CONTENTS

WHY THIS BOOK WAS WRITTEN

The authors have often been asked, "Why did you write this book?" It is not an easy question to answer. The project started a number of years ago when the authors used to meet and philosophize about the changing world, new life styles, and developing career options.

As these ideas crystallized, the authors began an intensive survey of the professional literature on new, emerging careers. ERIC, Medlar, and other computerized search techniques were used to gain information on emerging careers and to suggest additional places to contact. Very little career information on emerging careers was found in published books.

The next step was to write to more than 500 colleges and universities and ask the president or dean what new courses were being offered related to emerging careers. The responses from colleges were reinforced by materials for industries and from scientists in various disciplines. Newspapers, popular magazines, and newsletters provided additional leads.

It was only after many sessions devoted to reviewing and analyzing the data that the authors were ready to outline a book on emerging careers. The outline had to be revised when the authors saw that the material was so voluminous that one volume wouldn't suffice. The format of this first volume was developed to be augmented by the citation of hundreds of emerging careers in an appendix. At the same time, it became clear that the base of technology which underlies new fields must be summarized to provide a point of departure for intelligent career planning for them.

The breadth of interest in this subject has astounded even the authors. People want to know what to do with the rest of their lives and these volumes will provide a glimpse of emerging career futures. Hundreds of careers today did not exist 25 years ago and, conversely, hundreds of careers have been eliminated or greatly reduced in employment over that same period. A career planning goal is to hitch occupational aspirations to careers with a future. None are so bright as the careers which this book refers to as "emerging."

The careers of the year 2000 and beyond will change the occupational structure of our society and bring about challenges and options far beyond the imagination of the two authors. This book and later volumes in this series should begin to provide the basis for maximizing future opportunities.

INTRODUCTION

"Don't cross that bridge until you come to it."

"Live today, tomorrow will take care of itself."

"Nobody knows what tomorrow will be like so why try to prepare for it?"

These, and similar slogans have guided too many for too long. They guided the "Now Generation" which believed in living for the moment and taking its pleasures daily. People with these philosophies are depicted in the literature as happy and content in contrast to such serious types as Boy Scouts with their motto, "Be Prepared," life insurance agents with long policies conceived for those with fiscal responsibility, and career counselors asking, "where do you want to be 20 years from now?"

Yet, we know that the future is rushing toward us like an ocean wave, sending spray into the sky, crashing about us with astonishing force. The future arrives daily. We *have* to look ahead to see what's coming in order to be ready for its continuous tumultuous arrival. As one of the new "futurist" magazines puts it, "The past is gone, the present lost as it arrives. There is only the future."

One area where change is roaring down upon us most rapidly is in the world of work and its new careers. Not only are there literally thousands of completely new kinds of work, but we have constantly rising expectations of the role of work in life. In an older era work was something you did to make enough money to live. Work was work. Play was play. Today we believe that if you are in the right kind of work you should enjoy it. It should provide you with feelings of satisfaction, accomplishment, and self-actualization. This new philosophy, coupled with the fact that there are new and exciting kinds of work emerging daily, makes career selection more difficult today than in the past. But it also offers the prospect of a lifetime of happy accomplishment to those who are fortunate enough to link up with the right careers. And the clearest way to refute those sloganists who would live for the moment is to look at the millions caught in economic distress in the early 1980's as their obsolete jobs disappeared.

"The future belongs to those who prepare for it," proclaims a TV insurance advertisement. But author John Galsworthy said it better, "If you do not think about the future, you cannot have one." This book is about the future—your future. Whether you are still in school or college, in mid-career contemplating a change, or looking for a new occupation for your retirement years, with proper planning you can play a meaningful role in that bright new world that "futurists" are predicting.

Many of tomorrow's jobs are here already. We call them emerging careers—occupations demanding new knowledge and new skills, and offering new, exciting opportunities for those who are ready for them. This is a book about emerging careers, available now in small numbers, that will be available soon with far greater opportunities.

New careers are emerging so rapidly, and in some cases, changing so continuously that it is not possible to present for each new field standardized information on its advantages and disadvantages, education or training needed, working conditions, number of workers, typical earnings, etc. Many colleges and universities now offer creative courses leading to new careers. Other institutions, including industrial organizations, are educating and training personnel for new technical work. In the interest of producing this book, while the careers it discusses are still new, the authors opted to go with what is now known about each field. This book is not intended to be an "encyclopedia of new jobs and careers." Rather it is an index of starting points for your thinking. It is a book of ideas and new work and career facts designed to introduce you to new concepts about your own future. Resource sections at the end of chapters point the way to more detailed information sources.

New careers have been arising since humans first left the caves. Probably the first new careers to emerge in the murky dawn of prehistory involved communial food gathering, practiced largely by women, and hunting, practiced mainly by men. Before that, everyone spent full time finding and catching enough food on which personally to survive. Although this development is cited by historians to mark the first division of labor, it is the oldest example of two new careers emerging from one more general kind of work.

As civilizations began to grow, most of the people were still engaged in subsistence farming—growing a variety of plants, fibers, and animals to meet immediate needs for food, clothing, and shelter.

In the Middle Ages, emerging careers included those of various craft workers and artisans. They were able to make a living in the villages, servicing needs of the upper classes. The serfs continued to grow the food for themselves and their overlords, and to serve in military forces.

Another expansion in available careers occurred during the Renaissance. A whole class of craft and artisan assistants and guilds of them developed. Business, trade, and manufacturing were being expanded. Many worked at jobs which hadn't existed in the preceeding agricultural age.

Next, the Industrial Revolution vastly expanded the number and types of jobs and careers particularly in manufacturing and distribution. With booster shots from developing science and technology, this expansion has been going on ever since.

Just as new occupations and careers are constantly emerging, other fields are becoming obsolete. For example, hunting and food gathering in the wild became largely obsolete as societies began to practice agriculture with increasing success. One 19th century career of short duration was that of Pony Express rider, although vestiges reappear in today's courier and messenger services.

The elevator operator, the bowling pin setter, the home delivery milk driver, and hundreds of other occupations have virtually passed into oblivion recently. Many jobs done by hand are now done better and faster by machine. At one point in our history more than 50,000 women were employed in physically separating the yolks and whites of eggs. When they developed a machine that could do it better and faster, these women were let go.

This age-old process of emerging, declining and changing occupations is going on today. The barber of centuries ago is the surgeon of today; while the witch doctor of primitive societies is the precursor of the modern physician. In fact, jobs are changing so fast that many career guidance counselors predict that the average man or woman of the future will have six different jobs, though probably in related careers, within the work life span.

The newest edition of *The Dictionary of Occupational Titles* dropped some occupational titles because they had become obsolete. On the other side, it added many new jobs scattered throughout the many occupational classifications.

An emerging career is defined in this book as:
1. One that has become increasingly visible and distinguishable as a separate career area in recent years.
2. One that has developed on the job from pre-existing career

areas. Examples: legal assistant, community development worker, or teacher aid.

3. One that has become possible because of advances in technology or actual physical changes in our environment. Examples: home computers, solar energy research, satellite television, anti-air and water pollution equipment.
4. One that shows a growth in numbers of people employed, and in the development of education and training programs.
5. One that requires at least two months of special training or preparation before entering.

If you wish to play an active role in the bright new world which is arriving daily, you can start right now. Examine some of the new careers cited in this book and the changes in technology which created them and will create other new fields. When he accepted the Republican nomination for the presidency in 1952, Dwight Eisenhower said, "I hold that man in the right who is most closely in league with the future." Place yourself in league with the future so you may more fully enjoy the new age that is dawning. Your life style will be fashioned to a great extent by your choice of career. The parameters of tomorrow's careers are just now being determined. Grab a fistful of tomorrow with one of the new emerging careers in line with your abilities, interests, and personality.

Chapter 1

THE FUTURE AS THE EXPERTS SEE IT

"The Robots Are Coming, The Robots Are Coming," shouts the title of an article by Fred Reed appearing recently in *Next*, a slick new magazine devoted to previewing the future.[1] Robots are so new that no one is exactly sure how to define them. What is the distinction between special purpose automatic machinery and robots? Is an automatic washing machine a robot? The answer is no. The answer may be that to be called a robot, "the thing" must be capable of being programmed to do different jobs. In the automotive and aircraft industries, before a new model is put on the line, the factory is retooled. Retooling is expensive. It involves modifying existing machines, or building all new ones. A robot has an advantage over a riveting machine for example, because the robot can be reprogrammed to put rivets into new places according to the new design.

It's going to be five or ten years before robots are carrying much of the load in assembly plants says James S. Albut, roboticist-philosopher at the National Bureau of Standards. But the PUMA is already going to work in some factories. It is already changing the kind and amounts of work humans do. PUMA is an acronym for Programmable Universal Machine for Assembly. It is a little robot weighing about 120 pounds. The robots are definitely coming, and some of them are already here.

"The Computers Are Coming to Your House," announces an article in *The Wisconsin Alumnus*.[2] Computers have a long history going back to World War II, but the recent explosive progess in the

---

[1] Reed, Fred: "The Robots Are Coming, The Robots Are Coming," *Next*, Vol. I, No. 2, May–June 1980, p. 30.

[2] Pinkerton, Tad: "The Computers Are Coming to Your House," *Wisconsin Alumnus*, Vol. 81, No. 6, September/October, 1980, p. 10.

industry continues unabated. In the 1940's, room-sized computers used electromagnetic relays which required a lot of electric power. By the late 1940's and early 1950's, they were using vacuum tubes which didn't save much space but used a little less power. Transistors followed in the late 50's. These were the first solid-state devices and required much less energy to operate. Soon these too, gave away, to the integrated circuits we use today. With every change computers were becoming smaller and cheaper. By now, many school children have his or her own hand held computer. The end is not in sight.

In his article on the "Computers Are Coming" Professor Tad Pinkerton, Director of Academic Computing at the University of Wisconsin, used amusing pen and ink illustrations which made home computers look pretty much like the robots most of us imagine. But in his article Fred Reed said, "The friendly robot butler is not around the corner or staggering around in the future." But the robotics industry has ventured far into the production of home robots since that was written in 1980. There is a new household robot. It can be programmed to serve drinks, answer the door and do other household chores. More than 1,000 have already been sold at $8,500 each.

Professor Pinkerton speaks of home computers and the changes they will make in our lifestyles. "Computers are going to move into the home in a most satisfying way in what you might call educational or knowledge appliances. These are learning tools, not games. Many educational programs exist for these computers," and can be purchased on cassettes or disks.

Robotics and home computers are two of the newest fields you will hear more about in the next two chapters. The people already at work in them are pretty excited about the future. In their work, they get a clearer look at what will soon be commonplace. Our society is already being significantly shaped, economically, psychologically, and socially by the impact of increasing technology particularly in electronics, computers, and communication.

What will the future be like? What can we look forward to when many newly emerging careers are fully developed? For some answers we turned to the "futurists." They are a new emerging group of professionals who make their living by forecasting what the future will be like. Futurists, in general, tend to be excited by, and optimistic about, the new world that is emerging. Some of the more philosophic express a concern for the survival of our society. They stress that the future is not pre-determined. It is ours to create, and we need to be aware of this so we can move in the right direction to shape our future.

No matter what their particular persuasion, futurists all see a vastly new and different world ahead. Some of the things they agree on are discussed below—focusing on areas related to every day life in the home and community.

Population

Population will continue to grow, but less rapidly. In 1982 the U.S. population was 230 million. By the year 2030 projections call for 300.3 million people in the United States. There will be more older persons among us. The percentage of Blacks, Asians and Hispanics will continue to grow. This changing mix in our population will force manufacturers and politicians to pay attention to the needs of older citizens and minorities to a larger extent than at present.

The 1980 census shows shifts in the location of the population. There was migration out of the heavily populated, industrialized Northeast and Middle Atlantic States and from areas around large cities such as Chicago, Detroit and Pittsburgh. Population is moving to the Southwestern states and to Florida. There is also a trend from large cities to smaller cities and towns. Because of advances in communications technology, it no longer is necessary for large corporations to locate all their key personnel in one city. More people are discovering the advantages of small town life—avoiding traffic jams, high living costs, air pollution, and crime. More people are also working out of their homes. This may be one of the most significant trends of the future.

Health

People will be living longer. As around July 1981 there were 36,589,000 people 60 and older. This figure will grow to 70.3 million by the year 2030. Medical science will also make longer lives more active and pleasant. The numbers and types of health care specialists at all levels have increased as medical science has advanced. All kinds of new "spare parts" banks, including more than 70 eye banks, already exist. Many scientists predict the use of electronically operated, artificial hearts. One prominent biologist believes that future generations do not need to die: people, who can afford it, will have their bodies frozen and reawakened when the disease or age to which they succumbed, has been conquered. Cryogenic technicians already exist in a number of communities.

Instead of long hospital stays, the chronically ill will go to outpatient clinics. Dying patients who need professional care will get living and sympathetic care in hospices that will meet their medical, emotional and psychological needs and the needs of their families.

Medical costs will continue to rise prompting some sort of national health insurance so that this new health knowledge may be more fully utilized. Health maintenance programs, which place emphasis on prevention, are expected to gain much greater attention.

Computerized Homes

Home computers are just now beginning to appear on the market in quantity and variety. They will bring the whole world, and a large percentage of its knowledge, to any user's living room. New learning networks will make learning much more available, while recreational networks will usher in an endless range of entertainment. Shopping and banking may be easily accomplished without leaving the house. The house will be managed by numerous new sensors which automatically control the heat, humidity, turn on the oven, etc.—once they are programmed to do so. The number of choices available to the average person may become almost overwhelming.

Many more people will work at home. They will hold business conferences through closed circuit television, and send reports and messages from home-based computer terminals.

There will be more devices to help the handicapped including the blind to communicate, move around, and in general take part more fully in our daily life.

Obsolescence

Faster and faster obsolescence will be a fact of life in the future. The space shuttle Columbia which made its first successful space flight in 1981 will be out-moded by the "second generation" space shuttles. These are already on the drawing boards, although today three "first generation" shuttles remain to be completed and launched.

Those who purchased early models of home computers, have already found that newer models are more complete, more capable and smaller. Years ago, the first portable recorders used electromagnetized spools of wire. One of the authors, who was teaching at the time, saw these models come and go within the span of three short years. They were replaced by tape recorders, and shortly after that by cassette recorders. The early models were not standardized, could not be repaired, and became completely useless.

The rapid advance of technology will cause such obsolescence to occur ever more rapidly. We are now able to measure time in billionths of seconds. There are machines that can perform two million computations in seconds. This is taken for granted in the missile program where precisely exact timing is necessary all along the line. Perhaps obsolescence is one of the prices we pay for our increasing control of time.

Travel and Transportation

Travel and transportation will continue to develop. As one futurist said, "The American love affair with the automobile is here to stay until infinity because of the convenience and privacy it alone offers."[1] This points to more small, fuel efficient cars, more electric cars, and more diesel-driven vehicles. More people will rely on public transportation for longer trips, usually travel by air. Crowded airport check-in counters and parking lots will not diminish the traveler's ardor as wide-bodied planes accommodate more and more passengers in a single flight. International travel to new exotic places will become possible for many more average American people through group tours and package plans.

Futurists see some improvement in luxury, inter-city bus service, particularly along the Northeast Corridor from Boston to Washington. Passenger train service will probably continue to decline. Urban transportation systems will grow only on the basis of available tax revenues rather than needs.

Leisure

The average American of the future will probably work fewer hours per week. He or she may spend as much time or more in bureaucratic hassles, or being tied up in traffic jams. Nevertheless, a boom in the recreation industry is predicted. All sorts of delightful new theme parks will be available. The rage for family camping will continue although travel will become increasingly expensive. Many camping families will be forced to seek sites close to home. The National Parks will become more crowded, to the point of requiring far in advance reservations just to be admitted.

---

[1] Joel Norman of the Stanford Research Institute quoted in *U.S. News & World Report*, October 15, 1979.

Mobile homes and recreational vans will continue to be popular, though they will become smaller and more fuel efficient. The affluent American's dream of a vacation house in the mountains or at the shore won't diminish but high costs may alter it. More people will invest in time shared condominiums—a concept that gives families the use of resort homes for a couple of weeks each year for a one-time payment of from $10,000 to $25,000 and shared maintenance expenses.

Participatory sports will gain a new emphasis as our understanding of the need for fitness increases. Women will increasingly participate in professional sports. Gambling centers like Las Vegas and Atlantic City will multiply. Eating out will be increasingly popular as more and more women work, and more families have two paychecks. Leading the increase are the fast food chains which have been growing at a rate of 12 to 15 percent a year.

On an every day basis, the average American home should have a sophisticated home entertainment center which can play cassettes featuring favorite movies or television shows. They can also show a wide variety of education programs. Music may be composed by computers. It may be as different from "traditional" music as a harpsicord recital is from the sound track of *Star Wars*.

Social Relationships

Just as the types of work have been changing since the beginning of time, so also have our relationships with our families, friends, communities, employers, and other parts of our society. It is quite normal for human relationships to grow and change. We change also in our expectations for such institutions as schools, churches, hospitals, and local, state, and national governments.

Recent publicity has highlighted apparent changes in family patterns. A major contribution has been the movement of so many women into full-time jobs and careers. There has been a dramatic rise in the divorce rate as women claim their right to participate more fully in the economic and political life of our country. At the beginning of the '80s it was predicted that one of every two marriages will end in divorce. The prediction is almost true today in California. Many young people defer marriage, preferring to live together in a less obligating relationship.

Many two-income families are pioneering new ways to enjoy the personal and social values of family living, while at the same time allowing each marriage partner to develop a full-time fulfilling career.

In commenting on the family's chances of survival in the 1980s, a headline in *U.S. News and World Report* (October 15, 1979) states, "A difficult decade lies ahead for the nation's households. Major adjustments will come, but in the end, families are expected to endure."

The individual role in society is undergoing just as radical and rapid change as is the family. New patterns for the future are emerging.

Crime and Violence

Many optimistic futurists tend to ignore the impact of crime on the grounds that somehow science and technology will solve this problem. No one can ignore the fact that serious crime in America has been increasing for more than a decade. However, criminologists claim that it is almost certain to subside in the 1980s. The reason: the census shows a decline in the number of teenagers and young adults who account for more than 50% of all arrests.

Religion

Some futurists predict a growing interest in spiritual things. This includes the organized churches, many of which have experienced recent growth in membership. It also includes the new "electronic church"—the charismatic religious leaders usually not associated with any of the organized churches, who build large followings through radio and television broadcasts. Many of these groups own their own radio and television stations and broadcast their messages nationwide.

The awakening interest in religion also includes astrology and the occult—in fact all the mysterious, not scientifically explainable aspects of human beings. This includes yoga, transcendental meditation and encounter groups, as well as the various religious cult groups usually centered around a single, personal charismatic leader. In some California restaurants seating is guided by the guest's zodiac signs.

Taken all together they represent a growing interest in the "other half of the human brain"—the half often ignored. Until recently it was believed that people used only the dominant half of their brains—the half where reasoning is centered. We reached our present technological level by developing our ability to reason, to think and be logical. The other half of the brain was considered so unnecessary that in the 1960s it was actually removed from some unfortunate children in an attempt to control their epileptic seizures. Now there is increasing evidence that the other half of the brain houses such evanescent factors as talent, intuition, pre-cognition, extra-sensory perception, conscience, religious and ethical sensitivity, and human emotion interactions.

Information

According to Peter Schwartz the new era which is just now dawning will be based upon information. Dr. Schwartz is the widely respected young head of Future Studies at *SRI International*.[1] He thinks the new era which is just dawning will be based on information. Information in its many forms will constitute our basic value—just as manufactured products was at the root of our value systems during the industrial era, and agricultural products in the agricultural ages. The storing and transfer of information is already a sophisticated science. Sales of highly specialized information from every kind of consultant, including the futurists themselves, will become the major product of the future. Schwartz considers all kinds of services as consisting essentially of the sale of specialized information—including everything from medical services, to television repair, to the local dry cleaner. The numbers and kinds of jobs in services are expanding more rapidly than in any other area.

One of the authors whose job was providing public relations service was trying to explain what she did to a friend from Turkey. During most of the explanation he wore a puzzled frown. Then he broke into a smile—"Oh, I see—what you sell then is nothing!" Like most merchants his concept of something you sell was limited to items manufactured or grown—something solid that had form and substance. Yet it is estimated that more than 80% of the workers of the future will be employed in the information industry.

Space Travel

For many of us, space travel sounds like science fiction. Yet the Space Shuttle *Columbia* has already made four flights and has now become operational. A space laboratory has already been operated successfully. Space mechanics are being trained today. Futurists predict that by the year 2000 there will be regularly scheduled space travel for passengers and freight to and from space colonies. Thousands of Earthlings may work at beaming solar power back to earth,

---

[1] SRI International, formerly known as Stanford Research Institute, is located at Stanford University, California.

or in manufacturing new drugs and other products in a gravity-free environment. Today we already have planetary scientists who are making space the future home of new generations.

But What If?

But not all futurists are totally optimistic. Some economic forecasters, some political pundits and military analysts predict economic world collapse, at least in the short run. They wonder if we can get beyond such a catastrophe. We must find some solutions to many of the horrendous problems that face us today: How to provide enough energy for everyone without destroying our environment? How to control our environment so that future generations also may enjoy and use it? How to manage world tensions and hostilities to avoid nuclear war? How to cope with domestic problems such as unemployment, inflation and a dozen other social issues. If things went really badly in any one of these areas, it could precipitate the worldwide economic and social collapse that lurks in the back of the minds of many. Anyone planning his or her own future should also consider these dark shadows.

Peter Schwartz is one futurist who is optimistic but he is also concerned with the survival of the human race and the planet we live on. In an interview with Joseph Spieler, Schwartz suggests an attitude which works for individuals as well as nations. In seeking to define the meaning of "crisis" he said, "I very much like the Chinese symbol for crisis because it consists of two characters that stand for different words—danger and opportunity. Crisis rarely occur without an opportunity for change and growth, but if you fail to grow from them, you face real dangers—of collapse, distruction, death." The interviewer summed up his guiding philosophy—"The future is not predetermined. Whatever the future—it is definitely ours to create from the present."[1]

Tomorrow's Jobs

To learn what is already happening to the world of work, one need only read the *New York Times* annual Career and National Recruitment Supplement. A recent annual issue not only contained many

---

[1] Spieler, Joseph: "After the Recession," *Quest/80;* The International Cultural Foundation, 1133 Avenue of the Americas, New York, N.Y. 10036; September 1980, p. 26.

perceptive articles, but included more than 100 advertisements. Well over half of these were placed by companies in computers, computer software, computer services, communications, aerospace, and research and development.

One ad headlined "In the Tomorrow-Minded World of Martin Marietta Aerospace, America's Future is on the Agenda Today." Martin Marietta went on to list two dozen areas where it was seeking people for "entry-level growth positions"—including Software, Propulsion, Structures, Dynamics, Stress, Mission Analysis, Test, Thermodynamics, Mechanisms, Quality, Materials, Product Development, Industrial Engineering, Integration, Systems, RF Systems, Data Handling, Payloads and Sensors, Logistics, Safety, Guidance and Control, Communications, Power Systems, and Manufacturing.

General Electric, "the company that's applying computer technology on a superscale," advertised openings at various experience levels in "Hardware: Computer Designers, Electronic Designers, Project Engineers/Managers, Materials Flow Specialists, Digital Systems Engineers, Installation, Service, Program Planning, Product Engineering, Mechanical Engineers (Applications Development)." In "Software:" it had openings for "Systems Analysts/Designers, Engineering Programmer/Analysts, Data Base Designers, Information Systems Managers, Systems Programmers, Product Software Engineers, CAD/CAM Designers, Education/Training Specialists."

RCA Astro-Electronics, known for its historic trademark of a quisical dog looking into the speaker of a Victrola, needed ten different kinds of specific systems engineers, five kinds of mechanical engineers, six kinds of communications design engineers, plus a dozen or so other kinds of specialized engineers.

A number of chemical companies and drug companies courted the services of the highly trained. For example: "surface chemists, polymer chemists, and analytical chemists." Just becoming a simple chemist or an engineer is no longer enough to land the really good jobs in the eighties.

A developer of synthetic fuels needed a "Coal Liquifaction Scientist," a "Reactor Systems Technology Engineer," a "Computer Scientist," and a "Process Engineer–Waste Water Systems."

Several high-powered research and development organizations associated with universities, the Federal Government or private industry, advertised. The Plasma Physics Laboratory of Princeton University described in some detail eight different types of openings. It would seem to most readers that you have to be something of a specialist just to even understand the descriptions, such as:

"Circuit Design Specialist

Senior E E with strong analog and digital circuit design skills. Ability to react quickly and creatively in varied instrumentation problems. Background in data acquisition or telemetry helpful."

"Vacuum Engineer or Physicist

To work on high vacuum (10^{-9} tor) system of fusion research devices. Complete familiarity with Vacuum Science, related equipment including mass Spectrophotomers."

A number of banks, insurance companies and financial institutions, and even a few department stores like Bloomingdales and Macy's searched for executive talent. They also needed computer programmers and programmer-analysts, reflecting the fact that nearly all kinds of businesses are now computerized.

There were no ads from what we regard as the traditional basic industries like steel and textiles. This is not to say that there are no jobs in these industries. But many are contracting rather than growing industries as automation has cut into their employment totals.

In other publications, especially professional journals, we see many ads for relatively new fields such as genetic counselors, transplant coordinators, plant therapists, and numerous types of technicians. Tomorrow's newspaper "career supplements" may well include help wanted ads for specialists in robot behavior, in ocean hotel management, or in subquarkian physics—a few of many new careers coming over the horizon.[1]

Emerging careers are so new that the best place to learn about them is usually from newspapers or magazines. That is why this book so frequently cites them, rather than books which take years to prepare such as the excellent *Occupational Outlook Handbook*, published by the U.S. Department of Labor.

The occupational structure used in the *Occupational Outlook Handbook* grew and developed just as our industries did. For this reason it tends to lag behind the vast changes brought about by our rapid transition to an information based society. Occupational cate-

---

[1] For information on almost a thousand journals which list employment ads, see *900,000 Plus Jobs Annually: Published Sources of Employment Listings.* The title is taken from the estimated total number of vacancies which they list each year. This is available for $8.95 from the Garrett Park Press, Garrett Park, Maryland 20896.

gories are based upon the products of manufacturing, on traditional profession services such as law or education, and craft and service occupations. In the four pages the most recent edition of the *Handbook* devotes to "Occupations in Aircraft, Missile, and Spacecraft Manufacturing," it alludes to this problem.

> "Most jobs in aerospace manufacturing can be grouped into three categories: Professional and technical; administrative, clerical and related occupations; and plant occupations. Many of these jobs are in other industries as well and are discussed in greater detail elsewhere in the *Handbook*."[1]

Job Locations

Where will these new careers be located? Population follows the jobs. One reason for moving from one place to another is because you cannot find a job where you are. So you move to a new area which you hope will provide more opportunities.

The latest census figures, cited earlier, show a definite population shift away from some of the crowded Northeast and North Central States, to the South and Southwest. Only New York, Rhode Island and the District of Columbia actually showed declines in population. However, quite a few others reported growth rates to 5% or less. These include Connecticut, New Jersey, Pennsylvania, Ohio, Illinois, Indiana, and Michigan, some of whose industries have moved to the South and Southwest. In addition, some midwestern states were adversely affected by the ailing automobile industry which had laid off thousands.

There are still many jobs in these states, of course. What usually happens, however, when the job competition grows more severe, is that the newcomers entering the job market are forced to relocate to other areas with more opportunites. States which experienced more than a 20% growth rate in population were Arizona, Colorado, Florida, Hawaii, Nevada, New Mexico, Oregon, and Wyoming.

Concluding Thoughts

As you read what the futurists have to say about the world of tomorrow does it sound like science fiction? It does sound like science fiction, but there are important differences.

---

[1] *Occupational Outlook Handbook 1980-81 Edition*: "Occupations in Aircraft, Missile, and Spacecraft Manufacturing," U.S. Department of Labor, Bureau of Labor Statistics, March, 1980, Bulletin 2075; p. 503.

In 1870 Jules Verne, a French novelist, wrote *20,000 Leagues Under the Sea*, one of a number by Verne which established a completely new field of writing—science fiction. *20,000 Leagues* is about a highly mechanized, fully manned submarine and its many, fascinating exploits in the deep.

Verne created the whole story and described in detail this piece of underwater machinery, out of his imagination. While submarines had been thought of as early as the 17th century none of it was technologically possible at the time. One or two experimental models had been built, but it was not until the internal combustion engine became a reality, that practical submarines became possible.

20,000 Leagues Under the Sea was still popular reading at the time German submarines commanded the seas and devastated Allied shipping during World War I. People began to see science fiction as prophetic. No doubt the imaginations of some of today's science fiction writers are just as "on target" as Jules Verne's was. But there are two important differences between science fiction writers and futurists. Before making any predictions, today's futurist considers current and future needs, population trends, and the state of technology. Through statistics and with the help of advanced computers, a futurist can ascertain the growth rates and rates of change for any of the above. The second difference is that the futurist does not need to create a fictional plot or a cast of characters when he or she delineates the outlines of the world of tomorrow.

The prohetic vision of Jules Verne became reality in the early 20th Century. The predictions of today's science fiction writers, and futurists relate to tomorrow's realities. They have an important part to play in molding our expectations of the future, and in stretching our thinking so we are ready to accept, to utilize, and to enjoy tomorrow's world to the fullest.

In the 1930's a well-read comic strip was entitled "Buck Rogers in the 25th Century" and described how humans jetted through space to visit the planets and stars. Just to liven it up, to the obstacles created by such natural phenomena as the laws of gravity, a villian called Killer Kane made it rough for the imaginary, peaceful, space travelling people of this period. An interesting comic, thought people in 1939. Few would have dreamed that by 1969, a space vehicle manned by United States citizens would have landed on the moon.

Another popular cartoon feature described Flash Gordon who regularly journeyed to the center of the Earth. This is a prophecy which has yet to be fulfilled but may, like the submarine of Jules

Verne, have pinpointed a future area of exploration and possibly exploitation.

New careers will emerge such as Lunar and Mars mining, psychologists of robot behavior, ocean mining, or subquarkian physics. How do you, the reader, find out about these new emerging careers? Let's begin taking a look at the oldest of the emerging fields, the computer industry. This is a parent industry, which is involved in many other fields discussed later. Computers and their off-spring are making unbelievable progress in changing our world into the one the futurists have just described.[1]

---

[1] If you are interested in finding out how to become a futurist, or would just like to know more about the futurists' predictions as they develop, the central source is the World Future Society (4916 St. Elmo Ave., Bethesda, MD 20814).

Chapter 2

COMPUTER AND ELECTRONICS CAREERS

Computers

Many of the industries listed in Chapter 1 are branches of the fast growing tree of computer technology which began to explode in the mid-1940s. It continues to grow and change at such a rapid rate that some of the most common jobs it provided in the beginning are already obsolete. If you would like to become a part of the continuing swell of technological progress being made by the computer industry, there are many ways open.

Training:

One advantage of the "oldest of the new" is that computer training is now widely available. Short courses are offered by a wide variety of computer, vocational and business schools. Computer sciences programs are available through junior and community colleges and four-year colleges and universities. A good many universities offer work through the PhD and postdoctoral levels for those interested in computer research and development.

The Computer Operator:

The first step in learning about computers is to become an operator. There are several kinds of operating personnel including data typist, console operator, high-speed print operator, card-tape converter operators, and tape librarian. The names and kinds of these specific occupations change rather rapidly as the functions and capabilities of computers grow. For example, the need for key punch operators, once in great demand, is now declining.

The Computer Programmer:

The programmer writes detailed instructions that list in a logical order the steps the computer must follow to solve a problem. Computers can process vast quantities of information rapidly and accurately, but only if they are given step-by-step instructions. Because computers cannot think for themselves, programmers need to break down each problem into a logical sequence of very tiny segments.

Programs are written in special computer languages such as COBOL, FORTRAN, or BASIC. The programmer is also responsible for testing the operation of a new program and seeing to it that it is error free. This is usually called "de-bugging." Finally, he or she prepares a sheet of instructions for the computer operator who will run the program.

The Systems Analyst:

Next up the line comes the systems analyst. A systems analyst finds out from the supervisor or client, the specific nature of the problem the computer will be asked to solve. A very simple problem might be to ask the computer to alphabetize 500 or 5,000 names. There are standard programs already available for such simple tasks which can be purchased. Problems for which a systems analyst is needed may range from developing an inventory control system, to forecasting sales for an appliance manufacturer, or monitoring nuclear fission in a power plant. When the problem has been carefully defined, and when any additional needed information has been collected, the analyst outlines a system for the client. If it is accepted, the systems analyst translates the logical requirements of the system to the capabilities of the computer. He or she writes a "problem description" which includes specifications for the programmer to follow. The analyst works with the programmer to "de-bug" the program.

Because the work is so varied and complex, analysts usually specialize in either business or scientific and engineering applications. Some 15 to 20 percent of all systems analysts jobs are in research and development, helping create new technology. They may work for computer manufacturers, or for high-technology companies (like Bell Laboratories) or for the aerospace industry. Such people are often recruited out of college. They start as programmers and move up to analyst in a few years. They may have financed part of their own higher education by working as an operator or programmer while in school. The stages one may move through from systems analyst in a computer research and development organization, are as varied as the ever increasing number of applications to which computers are being put in our society.

The majority of systems analysts, however, are not in research and development. Rather, they determine ways to use existing technology in businesses as varied as the manufacturing of blue jeans, selling by mail order, processing foods, or banking. In truth, all types of businesses are either competely computerized, or in the process of becoming so. Like secretarial skills taught in business schools of the past, computer skills may be applied almost universally.

The Job Outlook:

The job outlook for computer operators, programmers, and systems analysts will continue strong into the foreseeable future. In early 1980, the average starting pay for a systems analyst was $17,000. After five years experience he or she averaged $28,000 annually. Working conditions are generally comfortable. Computers require carefully air-conditioned rooms, but sometimes the noise level becomes quite high. One disadvantage of the field is that the career path to higher management has not yet been clearly worked out. Usually the most realistic career goal of a systems analyst is to become head of the computer division. However, since more and more business functions depend upon computers, and since top executives will continue to need more expertise in this field, it is only a matter of time until the way to the top management positions becomes clear for computer experts as well as for those from other areas.

The corporate world is increasingly selecting people with a BS in business or with an MBA. Such graduates generally have taken computer science as a part of their core curriculum. Upwardly mobile systems analysts might be well advised to pick up management training courses as a part of their continuing education.

Home Computers

The first computers were huge machines used by a few gigantic industries. The training just described was developed for use with them. The relatively inexpensive, easy-to-use personal computer is the segment of the industry that analysts expect to show the fastest growth over the next five years. These minicomputers are being used by an ever increasing number of small businesses as well as by individuals and families. In 1980 it was predicted that the minicomputer market would reach $2 billion annual sales by 1984. It already reached that figure by 1982. Eight or ten companies are now manufacturing home computers and home computer software in a major way.

The story of one of the three companies which dominate this field is *Apple Computer, Inc.*, which can be an inspiration to any who aspire to be among the creators of tomorrow's world. This company was founded in 1976 by two college dropouts who raised $1,500 by selling an aging Volkswagen bus. They set up a shop in their garage and spent six months designing their first Apple Computer. The co-founders, Steven P. Jobs and Stephen G. Wozniak, were only 21 and 26 years old at the time.

Since 1977, its first full year of business, Apple Computer has ridden the flood tide of this swelling industry. Its sales that first year totalled $2.7 million. They rose to $15 million the following year, and to $75 million in 1979. Their total was around $200 million in 1980[1] —in 1981, $334.9 million. Projections for 1982, made in the third quarter, were $589 million.[2]

Just as with hand-held calculators, the cost of home computers is decreasing as the industry expands and gets into mass production. Already home computers are within the financial capabilities of many families. Of the three leading companies, charges for the basic terminal unit are $900 to $6,000 for TRS 80 systems manufactured by Tandy Corporation and distributed by their Radio Shack retail outlets, $995 to $1,995 for the PET personal computer manufactured by Commodore International, and $2,000 to $2,600 for an Apple II.[3]

But just what does a home computer do for you? To find an answer Susan Hasslet took an Apple II into her home and tried it out, as reported in *Quest* (July/August 1980). The first step after learning the computer's vocabulary of basic operating commands (the language is called BASIC) was to practice operating it. A variety of software programs or games are available now. The programs range from classic barroom version of "Sink the Cruiser" to "Color Math" a simple addition drill for elementary children. Three impressive software programs Miss Hasslet reported, were created specifically for the Apple II. One is a game called "Three Mile Island." It's objective

---

[1] Parisi, Anthony J.: "Technology—Elixir for U.S. Industry," *The New York Times*, Section 3, Business, Sunday, September 28, 1980, p. 1.

[2] Chase, Marilyn: "Apply Computer Says Profits Rose 70% in Quarter, 50% in Year as Sales Surge," *The Wall Street Journal*, Thursday, October 1, 1982, p. 56.

[3] These 1982 prices for the barest minimum package give you some idea but they are hard to compare because each company may include a slightly different array of features in its basic package. These prices would not include a printer, and few if any software programs. Without an additional expense, one could not take advantage of much of what the computer offers.

is to keep a nuclear power plant running safely and efficiently while supplying electric power to customers and returning a profit. A second program called "Forte" allows you to compose music on the computer. The third called "Supertalk" translates languages. Miss Hasslet describes several other kinds of information sources that a home computer can put you in touch with.

Through a hook-up with a Telecomputing network organization, you can tie into a national electronic mail systems, the United Press International general Wire Service, the *New York Times* Summary, The *New York Times* Consumer Data Base, a travel service, business data, applied programs (in science, engineering, and language), educational programs for children, personal finance programs, and a large assortment of computer games as well as biorhythms, horoscope, and wine tasting information. To avail yourself of all these services would cost more than the original hardware. Computers may also be used to send communications and to keep in touch with others with computers.

These are just some of the many things a home computer could do for you and those in your household. Very likely home computers will become increasingly effective in the drive to conserve energy. Already prototype houses have been developed which use computer-operated equipment to make maximum use of the available energy from the earth, sun, and wind. A large home (5,300 square feet) in Greenwich, Connecticut, makes use of all three energy systems, managed by an Apple Computer. Details of this particular house appear in Chapter 7 which discusses solar heating and cooling.

Computer Software

When computer manufacturers first began to sell their wares to business and institutional customers, they quickly found it necessary to help their customers to adapt the computers to their unique needs. At first already available software (computer programs) were provided with the computer. Then the computer industry next found it necessary to develop additional programs to apply to more and more situations.

What they, and their customers, who employed their own programmers, very quickly found out was that preparing computer programs is a very labor-intensive and expensive process. This poses a particularly acute problem for the many small businesses beginning to buy and use mini-computers. Some first-time computer buyers spend 50% more for software than for the original hardware. This is expected to rise within five years to three times as much for software as for hardware. Compounding the problem still further is the fact that almost from the start there has been an increasing shortage of qualified programmers who can write computer software.

"The computer has to be told in agonizing detail, exactly what steps to perform to convert its raw power into useful applications," stated a *Business Week* writer (September 1, 1980). He defined software as "the long list of commands or instructions that tell the computer what to do." There are two kinds of standard or canned software. One is "systems software." This includes report generators, data base management, and other "housekeeping" systems. They are designed to make it easier for the customer to write and update software and computer files. The second kind is "applications programs" software. They automate specific business tasks such as payroll, inventory control, or billing.

The door was initially opened for the development of a separate computer software industry when IBM, the giant of the computer industry, decided in 1969 to charge separately for software and hardware. "Unbundling" as this process came to be known, underscored the value of software to people who had become accustomed to thinking of it as something that comes with the computer. Hundreds of small, independent software companies sprang up to meet the needs of computer users for developing and updating software. Many went into development and sale of standard package software, some do custom programming, and many do both. The increasingly serious shortage of programmers, plus an ever expanding need for software cause many observers to rate computer software as one of the major growth industries of the 1980s.

Manufacturers of computers clearly recognize the vital importance of speeding up the development of software. In an interview with a *Business Week* reporter one IBM Vice President for Marketing said, "Any hardware vendor that does not understand the significance of software is going to be a dinosaur."[1] A good many computer manufacturers are already spending over 50% of their research and development budgets on software. Just as the camera industry discovered years ago that their long-term financial future depended more on the repeated sales of film than on the cameras themselves, computer manufacturers are beginning to see that, as one put it, "We used to write software to sell hardware, but in the long term we now build hardware in order to sell software."

---

[1] *Business Week*, "Missing Computer Software," September 1, 1980, p. 48.

As each new model of home computers have come on line, they have become easier to program. More and more stock computer programs are available. New owners can now often adapt one of the stock programs, or create an entirely new program to meet their needs with little help from professional programmers.

The Job Outlook:

Although programmers are used in every aspect of the computer industry as well as in the organizations to which computers have been sold, the new and expanding computer software industry will be among the largest users of professional computer programmers. While there are some 300,000 programmers working in this country at the present time, the demand for highly skilled people to write software is 40% greater than supply. Competition for programmers is fierce.

One other question needs to be considered before one rushes off to become a computer programmer. What are the computer and the software industries doing to solve this critical roadblock to their continued growth? At least three computer manufacturers are working to develop a complete operating system for their microprocessors which will ultimately put entire software packages on a set of memory chips. It will then be possible for a customer to build a complete software system simply by stringing together sets of semiconductor chips. When this operating system is in place, it will be far easier to write programs that cause the computers to perform specific chores.

Another company is trying to cut software development costs by pioneering the concept of a "software factory." This divides up programming labor just as an assembly line divides automobile production into separate, specialized steps. A programming office determines specifications of the task to be automated. Another group converts those specifications into design requirements. Then programmers code and test each of the modules. They are finally passed along to a test group which checks the entire system.

Should either of these approaches make programming into a more efficient, predictable process, then the need for programmers might evaporate as rapidly as the demand for key punch operators did recently. But this doesn't look likely to happen for a long time.

Miniature Electronics

There are many more industries which share some of the technology developed in the computer industry. New industries also make use of technologies developed for use in space exploration, the aerospace industry, the electronics industry, and the communications industry, all of which have been enhanced by computers.

One of the most useful by-products of space exploration research to benefit the average citizen was the hand-held computer. The direct result of the drive to miniaturize and decrease the weight of spacecraft instruments, the hand-held computer (which has become less expensive and capable of more functions with each new edition), has lightened the average American's load of calculating everything from computing taxes owed to figuring out the proper amount to tip a waiter.

Right now we are beginning to reap an increasing crop of miniaturizations, which any person can own. An article in *The Washington Star*[1] was entitled "You *Can* Take It With You." Among the wonders it described and pictured were the following:

A miniature Video Tape Recorder weighing only 7 pounds. It is 10" square by 3" deep and sells for $1,000.

A portable typewriter/word processor which measures about 8½ x 11" and weighs only three pounds sells for $1,400.

A hip-pocket stereo cassette player which is only 3½ x 5¾ x 1-3/16 sells for $150.

A super-portable color TV with a 5" diagonal screen and an AM–FM radio can be had for $470.

A black and white, 3" diagonal screen portable TV not only includes an AM–FM radio but a stereo sound system and a tape deck—all for $380.

Lest you feel that most of the above fall in the category of expensive toys, the following items were also described which meet daily needs and also incorporate new technological features: A space heater, a portable coffee maker, a lunch box which keeps the cold things cold and the hot things hot, a portable electric generator, and a computer chess game.

A key to the continued expansion of the electronics industry as well as other high-tech industries, according to one expert, lies in increasing the supply of electronics engineers. Over the past decade,

---

[1] Brancatelli, Joe, & Peligroso, S.: "You *Can* Take It With You," *The Washington Star Magazine*, Sunday, January 11, 1981, p. 8.

the electronics industry grew 17 percent, but colleges increased their enrollments of electronics engineers by less than six percent.

Computer Graphics

Another good example of a technological spin-off from the space age is computer graphics—which illustrates how several new technologies are beginning to support each other. Three different groups are working in this field: computer graphics technologists from the computer industry, specialists working with teletext and viewdata, and scientists from the broadcasting industry. Technological developments have pushed them closer and closer. They share the common objective of bringing sharper, clearer visual information to viewers. The broadcasters are interested in presenting images and supply consumer information. Computer graphics technologists seek to present quality images but at less than todays expense. Teletext and viewdata (two systems presently available) have poor image capabilities but provide information inexpensively. When this triumvirate of technologies solves the remaining problems, clearer, sharper, and steadier television pictures will result. Speculations beyond this lead to such exciting possibilities as the wrist television, the pocket/communicatting/calculator, and the table top work station or home information center.

CAD/CAM

John Allan III was 41 and headed his own computer company— Productivity International, when in 1979 he said "I just lucked out. I realize I was at just the right time and place, got my Ph.D. when the first machinery was coming on line and realized I was a guy standing at the beginning of the curve. I busted my rear to stay on top and when I'm ready to retire everybody in industry will be doing what we've started today."[1]

Mr. Allan's company is dedicated to promoting CAD/CAM, short for computer aided design/computer aided manufacturing. CAD/ CAM is trying to bring intergrated, computerized efficiency to production systems for fields as diverse as designing clothes or building airplanes. Allan believes that CAD/CAM has now become so economically viable that manufacturers should be able to use computer technology to modify a part, design a manufacturing system, or auto-

---

[1] Peter Applebome, *New York Times Special Job Supplement*, Fall, 1979.

mate a production process. They then can use the computer to guide the manufacturing of the product. This does not sound much different than the PUMA described in the Introduction as a "little robot."

But before we move on to robotics, a final word about training.

If you would like to go into any of these new areas you need quite the appropriate education. Earlier we spoke about general computer training. But in order to go into many of these areas, you also need to know about electronics, radio, and television, or whatever. A good grounding in computer sciences is a good place to start since computers are involved in all these areas. As you begin to settle into your special interest area, take a few courses in related disciplines. You may be able to find an employer already involved in the area who may be willing to help finance your specialized training.

Jobs With A Future

The jobs listed below already exist. Many were described in the preceding chapter. Some are so new that they employ few persons at present.

Applications developer (mechanical engineer)
CAD/CAM designers (computer-aided design and computer-aided management)
Computer designer
Computer microprocessor technologist
Computer graphics operator
Computer graphics specialist
Computational linguist
Data base designer
Data base manager
Data base specialist
Data base typist
Demonstrator (business equipment)
Digital systems engineer
Education/training specialist
Electronic designer
Electronic die maker
Engineering programmer/analyst

Equipment analyst
Installation service person
Information systems manager
Library systems analyst
Materials flow specialist
Operator (high speed printer)
Operator (multi-language capacity
Program planner
Programmer
Program analyst
Project engineer/manager
Software support analyst
Software systems analyst
Software systems engineer
Software systems programmer
Systems analyst/designer
Systems programmer
Tape librarian
Teleprocessing engineer
Type designer

For Further Information—Some starting points

Adams, C. K. *A Beginner's Guide to Computers and Microprocessors—With Projects.* Blue Ridge Summit, Pa: TAB Books, 1978.

Carron, L. Peter Jr. *Computers: How to Break Into the Field.* Cockeysville, Md: Liberty Publishers. 1982.

rnational Comparison. National Re-
.W., Washington, D.C. 20418. $1.85.

and How to Get Them. New York:

SCIENCE, February 11, 1982, Back
husetts Ave., N.W., Washington, D.C.

treet, N.W., Washington, D.C. 20006.

Complete Job Hunting Manual for
nterspace, 1981.

hat Can She Be? Computer Scientist.
ooks, 1979 (directed at younger chil-

mputer Careers: The Complete Pock-
b Market. Rockville, Md: Sun Fea-

r-Related Occupations. New York:

and Data Processing. Princeton, NJ:

sociations of the United States and
, 14th Street, N.W., Washington, D.C.

ng to computers in this annual direc-
may be found in libraries.

ways Wanted to Know About How
terling Swift, 1981.

0 Town Center Lane, Suite 155, Cu-

Siewiorek, Daniel P., Bell, C. Gordon, and Newell, Allen. *Computer Structures, Principles, and Examples.* New York: McGraw-Hill, 1982.

Spencer, Donald. *Computers in Action: How Computers Work.* Rochelle Park, NJ: Hayden, 1978.

Vles, Joseph M. *Computer Fundamentals for Non-Specialists.* New York: AMACOM, 1981.

Women in Data Processing, PO Box 8117, San Diego, California 92102. (714) 561-4291.

Women in Information Processing, 1000 Connecticut Avenue, N.W., Washington, D.C. 20036. (202) 298-8000.

Working with Computers: A Guide to Job Careers. New York: International Publications Service, 1975.

Chapter 3

ROBOTICS AND ARTIFICIAL INTELLIGENCE CAREERS

Robots

From the very beginning, it seems, humankind has cherished the desire to create an artificial human. The idea can be traced back through time to prehistory, to mythology, to the folklore of creation. After all, God fashioned the first human out of clay, the Bible tells us, and then provided the breath of life.

Right from the beginning, good and evil have gotten into the act. Creation was God's prerogative, most primitive people thought. It would be wrong for scientists to create an artificial human, and if they did, the resulting creation would be evil. Out of this tradition come such stories as Frankenstein or the Golum. This tradition runs right down to today's science fiction which often features robots run amuck, or rebelling against their creators.[1]

Another thing which seems to have been true from the start, is that it is virtually impossible not to anthropomorphize about the robots we build. American factory workers who work along side of robots have come to think of them not as evil but as helpers. When one machine, dubbed "Clyde the Claw" broke down at a Ford Stamping plant in Chicago, its human partners gave it a get-well party. Chauvinism being what it still is, American factory workers tend to refer to a robot as "he," but at one plant in Japan, each of the many robots has been given the name of a female movie star.

We shall never know, of course, what triggered our ancestors to try to create robots. It could have been a need for companionship, or to

---

[1] The word "robot" incidentally comes from the Czechoslovakian word for forced labor. The Robot Institute of America defines a robot as "a reprogramable, multifunctional manipulator designed to move material, parts, tools or specialized devices through variable programmed motions for the performance of a variety of tasks."

improve their power base. Certainly it is valid to speculate that they simply wanted to create something or someone which could lift a part of the burden of drudgery from their backs—not far different from the creators of today's robots. Robots are being used to take over some of the dirtiest, most unpleasant and monotonous tasks in manufacturing. This may be the ultimate flowering of the benign robot tradition that brought us such delights, in the past, as "Pinocchio" and, in the present, R2D2 of *Starwars*.

Today's Robots:

What are today's robots really like? A writer in *Time* magazine (January 1, 1980) said, "They poke their 9-foot-long, rubber-sheathed neck toward the row of automobile frames (they are working on). From their beaks, a blinding shower of sparks streams forth. The escape of compressed air creates a loud hissing sound." *The American Heritage Dictionary's* number one definition for a robot is "An externally manlike mechanical device capable of performing human tasks or behaving in a human manner."[1] It is a definition our ancestors could have understood, but it bears little resemblance to the bird-like contraptions "craning forward, spitting sparks" which are found in many automobile factories. As the writer says, "A robot's basic function is not to look or behave like a human being but to do a human's work." Robots frequently consist of one or two long, mechanical arms or claws attached to a tree-stump of a body which is bolted to the floor. They may not look or behave much like humans but they score much better on being "capable of performing human tasks."

Among the tasks robots are performing in a variety of factories are welding, assembling parts, painting, stamping out metal parts, and transferring hazardous substances like plutonium. A team of ten robots build ceramic molds for engine turbine blades at a Pratt and Whitney automated casting factory. At one General Dynamics plant, robots select bits from a tool rack, drill a set of holes to a .005 inch tolerance and machine the perimeters of 250 types of parts destined for use in F-15 fighters. At Westinghouse's Bloomington, New Jersey plant, a robot takes 21 inch rods of yellow tungsten and distends them until they are long and thin enough to be used as light bulb filaments. At a Cheesbrough-Pond thermometer plant, robots can

---

[1] Morris, William, Editor: *The American Heritage Dictionary of the English Language*, American Heritage Publishing Co., Inc., and Houghton Mifflin Co., New York, 1971, p. 1123.

even extract the air bubbles from the mercury—an essential process in manufacturing thermometers. Robots make excellent mail carriers. The U.S. Government uses them in such diverse agencies as the Department of Energy, the Department of Commerce, the General Accounting Office, the U.S. Geological Survey and the National Science Foundation. Today more than 16,000 robots are working in factories and agencies in Japan, Europe, and the United States. Japan is the biggest user of robots with about 14,000. Japan is also outproducing the U.S. in manufacturing robots by five to one, although she imported her first Unimation robots from the United States in 1967.

In December 27, 1981 the *New York Times* reported estimates by the Japanese Industrial Robot Association, of the number of robots in use. The 14,000 in use in Japan were classified as "advanced" robots, and would probably correspond to our definition of what is a robot.[1] The association estimated for the U.S. 3,255, and another 2,000 in use in West Germany, Sweden and Italy. These figures agree substantially with those reported just a year earlier in *Time Magazine*. *Time's* figure for Western Europe included Poland, France, Norway, Britain, Finland and the U.S.S.R. which added another thousand.[2]

The modern robotics industry grew out of computer technology. With this new industry many new careers burst upon the scene with the momentum of a revolution. Indeed, it is called "the robot revolution" by many as it continues at the same top speed. An increasing supply of robot technicians and engineers is a prime necessity for the continued maintenance and creative growth of this new industry.

Unimation, Inc., of Danbury, Connecticut, is the largest United States manufacturer of robots. Founded in 1959, it was not until 1975 that it began to operate in the black. But since then!!! It's profits for 1980 were in the neighborhood of $42 million. Unimation's biggest competitor is Cincinnati Milacron. Others include AMF Versaton and Automatix, Inc., founded in 1979. As this was written, IBM and Texas Instrument were studying the advantages of getting into the manufacturing of robots by establishing robotics divisions.

The current explosion in manufacturing robots was made possible by the invention of the microprocessor. This is the same invention that led to the miniaturization and increase in capabilities for com-

---

[1] Comparative figures are confusing because the American and the Japanese definitions of robot differ. We classify many Japanese robots as "automated machines." They count some of our automated machines as robots.
[2] *Time*, "The Robot Revolution," December 8, 1980, p. 72.

puters. A microprocessor is actually a minicomputer so small that it can be fitted onto a silicon chip no bigger than a pea. This made it practical to use them as the brains to run robots. It also took a steady rise in labor costs to make robots economically feasible.

Robots and Social Change

The manufacturers who are using robots in U.S. factories, have been quick to praise their virtues as compared to those of the human workers they have replaced. "Yes, it costs a lot to buy a robot" (from $10,000 to $150,000), their reasoning goes, "but robots increase productivity." This is an era when our national productivity growth rate has been dropping compared to the Japanese and Europeans. Since we are in direct economic competition with the Japanese and the Europeans, robots will play a big part in our current re-industrialization.

What makes the robot so productive as compared to the average factory workers is that it can work three straight shifts, needs no coffee breaks, wastes no time at meetings or talking to fellow workers, needs no paid vacation, health insurance or other benefits. It is immune to government and union regulations on heat, fumes, noise, radiation, and other safety hazards as well as vested retirement plans. Robots do need regular attention and maintenance, however. They break down occasionally but, on the whole, their "down time" is much less than for their human counterparts.

Workers, in general, take a different point of view. So far there has been little complaining, even by those workers who have themselves been replaced by robots. This is mainly because the jobs taken over so far by robots are among the most boring and repetitive, hardest, hottest, dirtiest, and hazardous. Anthony Massaro, chief of robotics technology for Westinghouse, says that the size of the overall labor force is declining. In the next five years it will probably decline by another 25,000 workers due to attrition. There is no way to replace that many workers with young people coming into the market. "People joining the labor force these days don't want the dirty jobs," adds Massaro. Most labor leaders agree with this assessment and go along with the industry's proposed answer to displaced workers—to train them for jobs that do exist.[1]

Some labor leaders are already resisting the robot takeover. One United Automobile Workers district committeeman at a Buick plant said, "If we don't get smarter and start combating the machines, we

---

[1] *Time*, "The Robot Revolution," December 8, 1980, p. 78.

will be cannibalizing outselves and competing against one another for jobs."[1] A Chrysler metal shop worker pointed out the difficulty of defining suitable kinds of jobs to be taken over by robots. He said, "They say they are only going to put robots on boring jobs. But in an auto plant all the jobs are boring jobs."[2]

In 1981, the Japan Industrial Robot Association in Tokyo issued a report based on a survey of its robot industry. The Association predicted that if development continues as planned, there will soon be nurse robots to take care of physically handicapped persons, robots to sweep the streets, guide the blind, and fill certain jobs on fishing vessels. By the mid-1980s robots will be used in large numbers to spray insecticides on farms, spread fertilizer, inspect and pack eggs, milk cows, and cut lumber. Robots may also be used in planting and in ocean research.

For years, Japanese industry has been plagued by a shortage of technical workers. It is understandable that they should forge ahead in using robots to fill many laboring jobs. Many former laborers are being retrained to fill technical positions. The Japanese are not unaware of the future job displacement problems caused by robots. One Japanese industrialist predicts that "The day may come when many humans will be deprived of job opportunities."[2] But he did not think robots will affect the overall employment picture for another 20 years.

No one can be sure if labor will remain calm when the robots begin to take over the pleasanter, less boring or relatively safe jobs. This is already happening in the case of robot mail delivery and robots are already being programmed for certain middle management jobs such as inventory control. One thing is clear, in the short run, robots will cause vast changes in Americans occupational life.

The Job Outlook

The robotics industry gives every indication of taking off and moving ahead as fast in the next five years as its parent computer industry did before it. Wall Street analysts predict an annual growth rate of 35% through the 1980s. Forecasters in *Barron's* (June 2, 1980), predicted robot sales would range from $214 million to $500 million a year by 1985. New technology has already created new jobs. This was true of the telephone, electric, and radio industries earlier. It is true of the computer industry. But robotics is the first technology developed for the specific purpose of creating machines which replace human workers.

[1] *Ibid.*
[2] U.S. News & World Report: *The Robots Are Coming and Japan Leads the Way*, Jan. 18, 1982, p. 47.

The development of robotics has created jobs for scientists, mechanics, and technicians involved in designing, building, and servicing robots. One can see an increasing need for robots' supervisors in largely automated factories. But whether the development of robotics will create more jobs than robots displace is an unanswered question. Factory workers might well start to train to be on the side of supervising and maintaining robots instead of on the side of those replaced by them.

At present there are three general types of jobs available in the robot industry. Overall employment is small but will grow with increasing demand.

Planning:

Engineers are needed to select jobs a robot could perform based on a thorough knowledge of the robot and its capacities. This professional skill also requires understanding the tasks to be performed and the environment in which they are done.

Installation:

Technicians must install a robot and adjust it to the specific tasks involved. This person could be the graduate of a technical school with special interest in robotics.

Monitor or robot supervisor:

This person checks the operation of the robot on the line and keeps it supplied with any needed raw materials, such as wire for a welding gun.

A Word About Training:

"So far, in any case, we've created a lot more jobs than we've displaced," said Dr. Edward Fredkin, professor of computer science at M.I.T. "We are creating what is going to be an immense new industry."[1] So far, we have identified only two schools which are giving special attention to robotics—Massachusetts Institute of Technology and Carnegie Mellon University. However, most universities specializing in computer sciences probably offer what an upcoming roboticist needs.

What we have described so far relates mainly to what is happening right now in robotics. Projections for the future are breathtaking. Many already are in the research stages. Unimation, Inc. is working

---

[1] *Time, Ibid.*, p. 72.

to perfect a robot that can shear sheep, or pluck chickens. Robots to help farmers spray fertilizer and pesticides are on the drawing boards. One robotics company is advertising a mechanical sentinel to help prevent crime. The Naval Research Laboratory is developing a robot that can be sent aboard an unmanned submarine to repair crippled vessels underseas. CalTech's Jet Propulsion Laboratory is working on a robot to be sent out in space, which could explore rugged planets, look at rocks with its TV eye, and dig up samples with its shovel. Research in artificial intelligence is improving the micro-processor brains of robots almost daily. There seems no end in sight to the tasks of which they might be applied.

Artificial Intelligence

The frontiers for the computers and robotics industries have moved beyond creating mechanical counterparts for human workmen and women, to creating machines that think. The artificial intelligence scientists seek to understand what the brain does with its information—in other words they want to find out how the brain works. They are attempting to duplicate some of the brain's functions with machines. Computers can already duplicate many facets of the human memory function in their information storage and retrieval systems.

Artificial intelligence programs which focus on robotics have been undertaken at several research centers. These scientists are creating robots whose arms are linked to both television cameras and computers so they can react to changing situations on the assembly line. At Carnegie Mellon University, researchers are teaching robots to assemble electric circuitry.

Most of the robots scheduled for work on the nation's assembly lines are "dumb robots." They are capable of doing only those things they are specifically programmed to do, and in the precise order of the program. Move that pile of metal screws one inch to the left or right of where it is programmed to be, and the robot will continue to pick up nothing from that exact place, and insert nothing into the hole in the piece of machinery it is assembling.

The same tiny silicon chip which made possible miniature computers and other electronic devices, is responsible for the remarkable breakthroughs in the development of artificial intelligence. Three robot examples can be cited which reflect some thinking and less mechanical repetition. They are *Prospector, Internist*, and *Frump.*

The *Prospector*, an electronic assistant geologist, was built by S.R.I. International, working closely with professional geologists to codify the knowledge that a geologist uses. This has now been programmed on the appropriate software. Given a list of types of rocks and configurations present in the outcrop under study, Prospector lists the types of ore deposits that may be present and asks the geologist to rule out any he or she considers not applicable. The computer's questions become increasingly specific, and as the geologist answers, the computer rules out certain possibilities and comes up with a conclusion such as "there is possibly copper ore" or "there is possibly uranium ore."

Researchers at one oil well service company are developing a software program that can read data generated about geological formations reached by a drilling rig searching for oil-bearing formations. This machine can spare human geologists hours of drudgery required for examining all the data. It calls the attention of the geologist only when any interesting signs are encountered.

A program called *Internist* has been developed at the University of Pittsburgh. It focuses on internal medicine, studying how an expert medical diagnostician approaches a patient. Internist asks the doctor who is using it for special information about the patient: disease symptoms, items from the patient's medical history, laboratory and other test results, etc. As the data on the patient builds up, Internist (just like a real physician) discards some diagnostic options, and asks further questions about others. If one particular disease seems a possibility, Internist begins to ask questions which narrow it down or lead to its rejection. Ultimately a suggested diagnosis appears on Internist's screen. Internist can make available to young and less experienced doctors, the vast expertise built up over the years by the nation's top specialists who work with the computer programmers to develop the programs for each disease. The program at the University of Pittsburgh has codified the majority of human illnesses.

Programs to process and understand information—the written and spoken word are being created at Yale University's artificial intelligence laboratory. Yale has focused on how to represent knowledge in a computer so that the link between words and ideas can be made and lead, in turn, to logical conclusions. *Frump* as the program is called can already read short news stories and write perfectly grammatical, one sentence summaries in English, Spanish, and Chinese.

Several major computer manufacturers have set up research laboratories in artificial intelligence. Some are already manufacturing "smart computers." At least seven or eight new companies specializing in various aspects of artificial intelligence have been started recently. They are usually organized by professors or groups of professors who previously have been engaged in artificial intelligence research for universities. One such company works on the computer-fluency problem. A second seeks to provide low cost natural language software for personal computers. One specializes in computer-aided instruction. Another on vision-interpretations for industrial robots, etc.

Cognitive Science

The problems involved in programming computers, whether they stand in computer rooms or are encased in the mechanical machinery of robots, has forced scientists to try to discover how humans think. This has given birth to a whole new discipline called cognitive science. It is related to, but distinct from computer science and artificial intelligence research as it utilizes a wider cross-section of other disciplines. According to Morton Hunt, who wrote about "How the Mind Works" in the *New York Times Magazine* (January 24, 1982), this new discipline is an "amalgam of psychology, psycholinguistics, computer science, psychobiology, anthropology, and philosophy." Like the teams of researchers involved in the projects discussed above, progress depends on a number of persons from a wide cross-section of disciplines, working in creative and close cooperation.

One of the more interesting facts the cognitive scientists have discovered is that in solving a problem, the human mind goes through a process not unlike the one a computer must be programmed to go through if it is to be able to solve a problem. It involves breaking down the problem into tiny components. This may be a tedious job for a computer programmer who has also to program in all necessary factual information relative to a solution. But the human brain makes use of its data bank of relative facts and previous experience, and can move to a conclusion with unimaginable speed. A skilled diagnostician, for example, can often come up with a diagnosis after hearing only a few of the facts in the case. He or she usually calls this intuition, and has no idea how it occurs.

Cognitive scientists are fond of pointing out that the information capacity of the human memory is in the neighborhood of 100 billion bits of information. That is as much information as contained in a full set of the *Encyclopedia Britannica*. While the particular information needed cannot always be recalled by the thinker with the easy dependability of retrieving a bit of information from a computer's memory bank, it has one advantage. The thinker need not recall in which category the information was stored, a step necessary before information can be retrieved from a computer.

Training in Cognitive Science:

Research and development work on artificial intelligence is going on in the graduate schools of a number of our top universities including Carnegie Mellon University, the University of Pittsburgh, Stanford University, Massachusetts Institute of Technology, and Yale University. Frequently, teams of highly trained specialists work on artificial intelligence projects. Those dealing with the problem of creating a machine to duplicate the functions of the brain need to call on experts in the field of neurology, psychology, and sociology—all those whose functions deal with the nature and problems of the human mind. Those working in areas calling for reading, writing, and translation need experts in linguistics, and computer science. Those dealing with the creation of so called "expert systems" like *Prospector* or *Internist* work very closely with top professionals in the program's field. Needless to say, computer scientists are needed all the way, as well as other levels of competence in computers from the programmer on up.

Persons interested in cognitive science can usually find training in college and universities which offer computer science, information science, cognitive science or robotics, such as the schools mentioned above.

"Smart" Robots and Social Change

If the new thinking computers are becoming all that smart, why are we not putting some of them to work on designing a new society? In our present society, work is the essential way the average person contributes to his society. He or she receives pay in return. As artificial intelligence learns to take over ever increasing numbers and kinds of "mental work," more and more workers will be displaced. Dr. Raj Reddy, Director of Carnegie-Mellon University's Robotics Institute, said recently, "Currently, around 25 to 28 million people are employed in manufacturing in America. I expect it to go down to less than 3 million by the year 2010."[1] He adds that no one in a position of leadership understands what is happening or grasps the enormity of the problems coming upon us.

Years ago, as computers began to replace numerous clerical workers, most people were saying machines can never replace the highly skilled. Now it appears that with the aid of *Internist*, *Prospector*, and other intelligent machines yet to be developed, the only class of top

---

[1] *Business Week*, March 8, 1982, p. 75.

specialists which can never be replaced, are those capable of, and interested in working with computer specialists to write the specialized software programs. Presumably, top specialists can only become top specialists through long years of devoted service on hundreds and hundreds of cases.

Artificial intelligence is in the early stages of development. No one has said much of the possible social effects. William Stockton, writing in the *New York Times* ("Creating Computers That Think," December 7, 1980) did suggest that "If this new technology could be subverted, enormous evil could result." Computers that think are already here. Every generation of them that comes out is more capable of more complex types of thinking. They will pose problems but there is a brighter side. Stockton also said, "In the future, artificial intellgence could produce powerful assistants who manage information for us, reading books, newspapers, magazines, reports; preparing summaries, avoiding those things completely the computer knows do not interest us, keeping abreast of everything that happens in the world, seeing that nothing we really should know escapes us."

Jobs With A Future

(Note: Many types of computer occupations are used in the robotics industry. These were cited at the end of Chapter 2 and will not be repeated here.)

Artificial intelligence psychometrist (tester)
Cyborg mechanic
Industrial robot production technician
Robot attendant
Robot engineer
Robot programmer
Robot psychologist
Robot technician
Robotician (applications specialist)
Robotician philosopher

For Further Information—Some starting points

Barr, Huron and Feigenbaum, Edward A.: *The Handbook of Artificial Intelligence*, Vol. I; William Kaufman Inc., One First Street, Los Altos, California 94022, 1981.

Engelberger, Joseph F.: *Robotics in Practice.* New York: AMACOM, 1982.

Haugeland, John, Ed.: *Mind Design: Philosophy, Psychology, Artificial Intelligence*, Cambridge, MA: The MIT Press, 1981.

Hunt, Martin: *The Universe Within*, New York: Simon and Schuster, 1982.

"Industrial Robots Join the Work Force," *Occupational Outlook Quarterly*, Fall 1982, pp. 2–11.

The Institute of Noetic Sciences, Founded in 1973 by Dr. Edgar D. Mitchell, Apollo 14 astronaut, supports research and educational programs to expand human-kind's understanding of the nature of the consciousness and the mind-body link. This membership organization has a newsletter—*Institute of Noetic Sciences Newsletter.* For information write to the Institute at 2820 Union Street, San Francisco, California 94123.

Robotics Industry Directory, Technical Database Corporation, Box 727, La Canada, California 91011. An annual listing of manufacturers of robots and components.

Robotics Today—Calendar of Events, Society of Manufacturing Engineers, One SME Drive, Dearborn, Michigan 48129. Lists meetings, conferences, etc., dealing with robotics.

Turner, Charles H., *Maps of the Mind,* New York: MacMillan Publishing Co., 1982.

Check associations directories in the library for ones with an interest in robotics and/or artificial intelligence.

Check current periodicals in libraries for articles on robotics and artificial intelligence.

Chapter 4

ENERGY INDUSTRY CAREERS: OIL, NATURAL GAS, COAL,AND SNYFUELS

If we had to assign a birth date to the modern energy industry, it would be 1974. That was the year of the Arab oil embargo and the long lines at the gas pumps. That was the year when a number of things came together to convince most Americans of the following:

1. That we were no longer energy self-sufficient, as we had been until after World War II.
2. That depending for our oil on the politically volatile Middle Eastern countries was foolhardy.
3. That oil was an irreplaceable natural resource and would be totally depleted worldwide within the foreseeable future.
4. That industrialized countries like ours need to start immediately to develop alternative sources of energy.

The objective of making our country energy self-sufficient appealed to everyone who had waited in gas lines. By common consent, it was adopted as a national goal.

Theodore J. Gordon, President of the Futures Group, Inc., a management consulting firm which provides strategic planning and forecasting services, said recently, "By 2050 or so, our conventional petroleum reserves will have been substantially exhausted. Of course, they will never run out in the sense that there will be no more petroleum. It is just that the price of what remains will be so high that it will be impractical to burn it." How much time do we have before this happens? Mr. Gordon suggests that "The energy installations we make between now and 2030 or so can be viewed as temporary, filling the gap until new (solar energy) systems are available." Although reports often seem chaotic, the energy industry is taking a number of steps to get us through the next forty or fifty years until nondepletable sources of energy are developed.

Oil

First, the petroleum industry is developing new sources of conventional oil such as the great new fields in the North Sea and off the coast of Alaska. These are bringing in thousands of barrels of "new" oil daily. New oil is also being delivered from thousands of recently drilled off-shore wells in the Gulf of Mexico and elsewhere around the world. Finding and exploiting this new oil has been made possible by developments in engineering and technology. For example, Exxon Corporation drilled for oil in more than 4,000 feet of water off the coast of Australia. Exxon also drilled in the ice-clogged Beaufort Sea (a part of the Arctic Ocean) by first building artificial islands to serve as drilling platforms. (For more on off-shore drilling, see Chapter 9 on Ocean Industries.)

Second, the oil industry is working on many "enhanced recovery projects." On the average, only about a third of the oil in a given reservoir is recovered by older methods. New technology is making it possible to recover additional oil from many old, "exhausted" wells. Since the world price of oil has risen, it is now economically possible to extract more oil from old wells using modern tools and methodology.

The third method is through improving the refining of oil. Gasoline, diesel fuel, and jet fuel, which constitute an ever growing percentage of world demand, are refined most easily and inexpensively from "light crude." Light crude is easy to process, but is being progressively depleted. The technology in oil refining has been focused on ways to refine "heavy crude" into gasoline, diesel fuel, and jet fuel.

C. C. Garvin, Jr., Chairman of the Board at Exxon, wrote in the quarterly magazine, *The Lamp* (Spring 1981), "It will still be true that by the end of the century oil will remain the world's single largest source of energy." It is equally true that as we progress toward meeting our energy needs with nondepletable sources, the number of people working in the oil industry will decline.

Despite this long-range prediction, there are a number of fascinating new careers emerging in the oil industry. Fermoselle listed 37 occupations with the largest number of openings in the oil and gas industry.[1] Of course, they included the expected petroleum engineers and drilling engineers, but they also cited exploration engi-

---

[1] Fermoselle, Rafael: *Energy Occupations in Demand*, R. F. Associates, P.O. Box 5575, Arlington, Virginia 22205; 1980. (The book is out of print, but available in a number of large libraries.)

neers, reservoir engineers (oil), corrosion engineers, and "mud engineers." A mud engineer, incidentally, needs four years of college, a graduate degree, and several years experience. The oil industry also needs geologists, off-shore geophysicists, and exploration geologists. It hires drilling managers/supervisors, helicopter mechanics and pilots, plumbers, pipefitters, and diesel mechanics among others. If some of these fields don't sound very new, at least the setting where they will work is entirely new. Many are for crews of off-shore drilling rigs.

Up to a dozen new geophysical companies have recently been formed, based on the remarkable advances in seismic technology. They are assisting oil and gas companies to dramatically increase their odds of success in drilling for oil and gas. Known as the oil industry's "hired ears," geophysical technicians make use of the same technology and equipment that makes possible a better understanding of earthquakes and volcanic eruptions.

According to the U.S. Department of Labor, the oil and gas extraction industry will grow rapidly from 1980 to 1985 as a result of the expansion in exploration and drilling. The same agency expects petroleum refining to show little change through the mid-1980s primarily due to productivity improvements.

Natural Gas

Since 1978 oil and natural gas exploration has discovered vast new gas fields in the Rocky Mountain Region and the Gulf Coast of Louisiana. Their full potential has as yet to be determined but it seems clear that this energy source should last through the end of the century and possibly well beyond it. Since gas is frequently found in combination with oil or coal deposits, any exploration and development in those areas is also aiding natural gas. The natural gas industry uses essentially the same types of personnel discussed in the section above on oil.

Coal

Our country has one of the world's largest remaining resources of coal. The coal industry is already being called upon and will probably continue to be called upon to help meet our energy needs for the next fifty years or until nondepletable sources are much better developed. A National Geographic Society publication on the subject of *Energy* headlines the section on coal, *"Coal—Abundant Resource,*

Abundant Problems."[1] Burning coal improperly leads to air pollution and related health problems. Strip mining leads to environmental problems. It seems to be a national consensus that we will decrease our use of coal as soon as other sources of energy can take over. However, at the moment, it is a growing industry and the U.S. Labor Department expects its employment to rise by 39% by 1985. Federal money is going to the coal industry to help solve pollution and environmental problems and to make coal a more acceptable fuel. Research and development is quite advanced in coal gasification as discussed under synfuels.

The Job Outlook:

There are few particularly new and exciting careers emerging in this industry, which has for many years been highly automated. However, there is a special need for engineering geologists—for people who combine skills and knowledge in two different areas, both highly important to the coal industry.

Mineral economists are also in demand in the coal industry, just as they are in the oil, natural gas, and other extractive industries. Mineral economics, a relatively new field, is the study and application of both economics and management principles to the minerals and energy industries. It includes economic analysis, planning, and management. Specialties include market and commodity analysis, project and business evaluation, and operations research. Another area is mineral resource economics with emphasis on depletable resources.

Four universities offer specific training on the undergraduate and graduate levels in mineral economics. They are (1) the Colorado School of Mines in Golden, Colorado, which offers the largest graduate training program (about 20 students a year receive degrees), (2) Pennsylvania State University, which offers graduate degrees and also has a large undergraduate program, (3 and 4) are the University of Arizona and West Virginia University, which offer programs on both levels.

The field of mineral economics involves mining, petroleum, geology, economics, management science, and business. For those who choose this field, the pay is good and advancement may come rapidly since mineral economists are in short supply. Mineral economists also have the satisfaction of knowing that they are working on solving the problems posed by depleting natural resources.

---

[1] National Geographic Society: *A Special Report in the Public Interest—ENERGY Facing Up to the Problems*, Washington, D.C., February 1981, p. 63.

Engineering geologists and mineral economists are just two examples of many which illustrate that more and more of those who get to the top in today's world will have multidisciplinary training.

Synfuels

Synfuels are not so much "synthetic" as the name suggests, but are produced from mineral products from the earth or organic products grown on the earth.

Gasahol is classified by some as solar energy. Along with biomass, it uses sun-grown organic material to produce a fuel. (More on biomass in Chapter 5.)

Gasahol

Gasahol is the only synthetic fuel already being commercially produced in this country. It is used in both automobiles and farm machinery. Gasahol is a blend of 10% methyl alcohol and 90% gasoline. It is available now at pumps across the country, although you may have to hunt for one in your particular neighborhood. In a number of tests it has been found that cars operated on gasahol have performed better than on unleaded gas, with increased mileage and reduced carbon emissions.

Brazil took the lead in this field when it committed itself to an alcohol fuel economy. Its gasahol is 20% ethanol (ethyl alcohol) and 60% gasoline. Cars and trucks are already being produced which operate on pure ethanol. In the U.S. at least one large distillery, Archer Daniels Midland, is beginning to turn out ethanol. Numerous entrepreneurs are getting into the act. The Energy Research Institute in Colorado is developing small alcohol plants which can produce up to 30,000 gallons of methanol a day.

One thing that makes the prospect so exciting is that alcohol can be made out of almost anything. The Brazilians use sugar cane surplus and waste. Most of alcohol made in the U.S. uses corn and grains, often in surplus. Proponents claim that by using wood, food-processing residues, or surplus and diseased crops the nation can provide the 11 billion gallons of alcohol a year needed to convert our gasoline to gasahol.

"Jerry" Moody, who opened a plant recently in Wisconsin, makes his from a combination of corn and whey. Whey is a byproduct of cheese making and getting rid of it had become an environmental concern to the cheese manufacturers. They even pay Moody to take it off their hands. Another advantage that delights Moody is that

"Once you ferment the grain to get the alcohol, you have a high protein silage that can be transported to any of the nearby feedlots or dairy farms. Gasahol and methanol are in their infancy as synfuels."[1]

Methanol is another renewable source of energy since it is made from all sorts of plant and vegetable matter. The U.S. Department of Energy did assist those who wished to enter this field by helping them find financing, but some funding programs were limited or abolished under the Reagan Administration. It also made technical information and professional advice available for the asking.

Oil Shale

"Coal and oil shale, our most promising synfuels, are solids," states Dr. Kenneth Cox of the Department of Energy's Los Alamos laboratory in New Mexico. "This means handling enormous quantities of ore and building incredibly complex processing plants. These make synfuels much more expensive and more damaging to the environment."[2] Dr. Cox cited just some of the many problems that must be solved before we can extract much fuel from oil shale. Nearly two dozen oil companies have or are developing the plans for gigantic processing plants--mostly in Colorado, Utah, and Wyoming. They include Gulf, Union, Standard of Indiana, Occidental, and Tenneco. To spur their initiative, Congress in 1980 approved an ambitious synfuel goal of 500,000 barrels a day by 1987. This would mean that between 30 and 40 mammoth coal and shale oil plants, each costing from one to six billion, will have to be built.

Oil is produced from the shale by breaking it into small pieces (a process called rubbling) and heating it until the oil trickles out. Sounds simple until you realize that you only get 25 gallons of oil from one ton of rubbled shale, and the best shale for the purpose is often more than 1,000 feet underground. A barrel of oil as it is measured commerically may contain from 31 to 46 gallons established by law or usage. Despite the complexities of oil shale extraction, at least five commercial projects were developed in Colorado and Utah. Most used conventional mining techniques to bake out the oil in surface retorts that look a lot like oil refineries. One new plant being undertaken by Occidental Petroleum in partnership with Tenneco is expected to be in operation by the mid-1980s. Instead of bringing the rock to the surface, they will build retorts underground, heat the rubble there, and pump the oil to the surface.

---

[1] *The Cloverleaf*, October 1980.
[2] *National Geographic — A Special Report*, op. cit., p. 80.

All this activity, so far only in pilot projects or research facilities, has already caused mini-boom towns to spring up to accommodate a growing number of workers. Typically, demographers postulate that every basic job in this new industry ultimately will create nine secondary jobs directly related to the new industry. This does not include the basic construction workers. The oil shale industry is projected to create some 85,000 jobs (45,000 basic and 40,500 secondary). These figures include not only industry related jobs but all the new jobs created by the new communities in the birth of the new industry.

Tar Sands

Another significant source of synthetic fuel lies in the more than 550 deposits of tar sands already identified in the United States. These geological formations are similar to those of oil shale, except that the plant and animal material turned into oil is trapped in deposits of sand rather than rock. As with oil shale, it is expensive and difficult to extract the oil. In the Canadian province of Alberta, a large plant is already in operation. Our own efforts are still in the research and demonstration stage. The amounts of oil trapped in oil shale and tar sand in this country amount to more than 700 billion barrels of recoverable oil. This is four or five times the estimated oil reserves in Saudi Arabia, but it will not be easy or cheap to extract it.

Oil From Coal

The technology to convert coal to gas, to oil or to gasoline already exist. The Germans staked their claim to take over the world in World War II on the fact that they could fuel their lethal fleet of aircraft with synthetic gasoline. After the war a team of U.S. scientists was sent to recover the German synthetic gasoline secrets and brought back nearly 200 tons of documents for future study. For a brief time the U.S. Bureau of Mines built two coal liquefaction plants in Louisiana and Missouri. While they succeeded in making a very expensive diesel fuel that powered a locomotive, the whole project was dropped when vast quantities of cheap Middle Eastern oil began to flood the country in the early 1950s.

In 1950, South Africa began the switch from oil to synfuel by building a 10,000 barrel a day plant based on German technologies. In 1973 a second plant was begun in a different part of the country and is now in operation. A third plant at the same second location is now in the process of being built (1982).

The oil embargo of 1974 revived U.S. interest in oil from coal projects. Department of Energy scientists developed an $800,000 project in the 570 square mile Centralia-Chehalis Coal District of Washington State to test the commercial feasibility of underground coal gasification. An Exxon pilot plant was developed in Baytown, Texas in 1980 to convert 250 tons of coal daily into over 600 barrels of synthetic oil.

Government funding is making it possible for companies such as Gulf, Mobil Oil, Dynalectron Corporation, Texas Eastern, Ashland Oil, and W. R. Grace & Co., to plan and to build pilot synfuel plants in the coal rich areas of Kentucky and West Virginia. Significant outputs, estimated to be in the hundreds of thousands of barrels daily, are not expected from these plants until about 1990.

The Job Outlook

At the moment the synthetic fuels industry is in the experimental and demonstration stages. Only a limited number of highly specialized jobs are available in this field. Companies involved may need chemical engineers, process engineers, corrosion engineers, environmental engineers and design engineers and scientists such as chemists and physicists. For the present, while new plants are being put up, the biggest need will be for builders and building trades craftsmen. When the plants begin operation in 1984 or later, a whole new family of emerging specialists and technicians will be needed. One good way to get into the synfuel business would be to go to work for one of these companies. They may even be willing to train you for one of the new specialties. As an insider you will be in a better position to assess what may be needed to enter into and move up in this brand new industry aborning.

The petroleum surplus and a drop in oil prices which developed in 1981 had an effect on the speed at which the synfuels industry will develop. If oil prices keep rising, the multi-billion dollar synfuels industry is on its way. If prices stabilize or fall, and especially if the massive government support is curtailed, the fledgling synfuels industry may be stunted in its growth. The recession of 1981 led to deep cut-backs in planned research and development projects by both the Federal government and private industry.

Jobs With A Future

Chemical engineer (oil, synfuels)	Environmental engineer (all)
Corrosion engineer (oil)	Equipment engineer (all)
Diesel mechanic (all)	Exploration engineer (all)
Drilling engineer (oil)	Exploration geologist (all)
Engineering geologist (all)	Geologist (all)

Geophysicist (all)

Instrument control analyst (oil)

Landman (oil)

Land manager (oil)

Material resources economist (all)

Mineral economist (all)

Mud engineer (oil)

Petroleum engineer (oil)

Physicist (all)

Pipe fitter (oil, gas, synfuels)

Plumber (oil, gas, synfuels)

Process engineer (all)

Production engineer (all)

Pumper (oil)

Reservoir engineer (oil)

Stripping operator (coal)

Tractor operator (coal)

For Further Information—Some starting points

American Association of Petroleum Geologists, Inc., P.O. Box 979, Tulsa, Oklahoma, (918) 584-2555.

American Association of Petroleum Landmen, 2408 Continental Life Building, P.O. Box 1984, Fort Worth, Texas 69101, (for career information) (817) 335-9756.

American Institute of Mining, Metallurgical, and Petroleum Engineers, Inc., 345 E. 47th Street, New York, New York 10017, (212) 644-7695.

American Petroleum Institute, 2101 L Street N.W., Washington, D.C. 20037, (202) 457-7000.

Careers for Engineers in the Mineral Industry. Society of Mining Engineers of AIME, Caller Box D, Littleton, Colorado 80127.

Careers in Exploration Geophysics. Society of Exploration Geophysics, P.O. Box 3098, Tulsa, Oklahoma 74101, (805) 942-9574.

Careers in Petroleum Engineering. Society of Petroleum Engineers of AIME, 6200 N. Central Expressway, Dallas, Texas 75206, (214) 361-6601.

Directory of Geoscience Departments. American Geological Institute, 5205 Leesburg Pike, Falls Church, Virginia 22041, (703) 379-2480. Lists colleges and universities with programs in geoscience.

Energy and Jobs for the 80's. The National Urban Coalition, 1201 Connecticut Avenue, N.W., Washington, D.C. 20036, (202) 331-2400. $5.00.

Energy Education Catalog. American Council on Education, Publications Unit, Suite 30, One Dupont Circle N.W., Washington, D.C. $15.00. A joint project of the ACE and the Academy for Educational Development, this directory lists around 250 energy education programs in colleges and universities.

Fermoselle, Rafael, *Energy Occupations in Demand.* R. F. Associates, P.O. Box 5575, Arlington, Virginia 22205, 1980. (Out of print.)

Geophysics: The Earth in Space. American Geophysical Union, 2000 Florida Avenue, N.W., Washington, D.C. 20009, (202) 462-6903.

Independent Petroleum Association of America, 1101 16th Street, N.W., Washington, D.C. 20036, (202) 857-4722.

Manpower in Energy-Related Activities—A Summary and Review of Recent Studies. A technical report to aid counselors and manpower planners prepared by the U.S. Department of Energy. Copies are available from the National Technical Information Service, U.S. Department of Commerce, Springfield, Virginia 22161 for a fee.

National Coal Association, 1130 17th Street, N.W., Washington, D.C. 20036, (202) 628-4322.

Penetrating New Frontiers with Minerals Engineers. Society of Mining Enginners of AIME, Caller Box D, Littleton, Colorado 80127.

Professional Energy Careers. U.S. Department of Energy, Office of Public Affairs, Washington, D.C. 20585, 1979.

Chapter 5

ENERGY INDUSTRY CAREERS: NUCLEAR FISSION AND FUSION

Nuclear Fission

There were 73 nuclear power plants in operation in this country in the early 1980s. They produced electricity, 55,000 megawatts worth, or 12% of our national electric power need. Without these plants we would have to import 1.5 million more barrels of oil a day. By 1990 there will be 166 nuclear plants in operation, according to the American Nuclear Energy Council. They will turn out 160,000 megawatts of electric power, or from 25 to 50 percent of our total need. By the year 2000 or just beyond, 50 percent of our electric power need could be supplied by nuclear plants. Even the 25 to 50 percent level by 2000 means an increased number and variety of jobs in the nuclear power generation industry.

In the nearly 40 years since the nuclear explosions which ended World War II, national attention has focused on how to convert this might force into production of energy. Peaceful atomic energy research continued in the same laboratories which had developed the bomb. It was not until the Eisenhower administration, however, that atomic energy got a boost through the "atoms for peace" program. Three years after the passage of the Atomic Energy Act of 1954, the first atomic power plant was brought on line at Shippingsport, Pennsylvania. By 1965 there were 12 plants in operation, and by 1975 there were about 56.

With the dawning recognition that the world's oil supplies were running out, important decisions were made in board rooms of utility companies all across the country. Many opted to go with nuclear energy to help meet our ever expanding need for electricity.

The oil embargo of 1974 focused public attention on the need to develop alternate sources of energy. For a brief time, we seemed to be interested in accelerating atomic energy developments. In 1974, the number of power companies seeking licenses to develop new atomic power stations began a sharp decline. They were becoming disenchanted by three stubborn problems.

One was an ever increasing amount of bureaucratic red tape involved in obtaining the many licenses, permits, and clearances needed from every government jurisdiction from the township to the federal. This problem had grown rapidly since the first plant had been opened at Shippingport in 1957. It had moved from planning to operation in relatively few years. Today, the Japanese and Europeans are still able to bring in a new plant in six years. An American company, by contrast, has to allow 15 years.

A second deterrent is opposition from anti-nuclear groups who are growing increasingly skillful at using every means available through the courts, government regulatory agencies, and the mass media to delay or prevent construction.

A third problem is that of safely disposing of radioactive waste.

Utility boards of directors began to reassess the advisability of 15 years of very heavy cash outflow, before one kilowatt from a new nuclear plant could be sold. When the first serious accident at a nuclear power plant occurred in 1979 at Three Mile Island, there were 72 plants in operation, 94 others under construction, and 40 on order. According to *U.S. News and World Report* (August 13, 1979), "The Three Mile Island incident also has touched off an agonizing reassessment of nuclear energy in Congress, the White House, government agencies—and most importantly in the utility company board rooms."

Comparing the above 1979 figures with those of 1981 from the American Nuclear Energy Council, we added only one more plant in two years. Another 72 have received construction permits, and 11 are in the planning stages. There have been cancellations of a number of orders placed with manufacturers such as Westinghouse and General Electric.

The development and continued use of atomic power is considered by most futurists, as well as the industry itself, as being necessary if we are to meet our energy needs for the next 30 to 50 years, or until new systems of renewable energy from the sun or from the fusion reaction are developed. Atomic energy as a source of power will continue to be developed into the 21st century. It's technology will be advanced and improvements made.

As with all new technologies, final refinements and improvements can only be made as they are put into operation. The highly publicized problems which nuclear power plants are experiencing represent a phase in their technological development. Compared to the number of plants in operation, most of them with more than one reactor unit, the number of problems has been minimal. This bodes well for atomic power's ability to fulfull its role in meeting our energy needs. Because of what the public considers to be news, we never hear about the many smoothly running atomic power plants, or about how they are lowering energy costs in the areas where they operate.

The Job Outlook:

Construction of new nuclear energy plants will continue for at least another two decades. Construction requires thousands of skilled workers—everything from boilermakers, pipefitters, welders, and sheet metal workers, to office workers, laborers, and truck drivers. Some of these like the boilermaker welders and pipefitter welders must be nuclear certified. While most of these are not new skills, they will be performed in new settings. One recent estimate is that 91,720 skilled workers, laborers, and drivers will be needed. This is down slightly from the needs for 1980 and probably reflects frustration with obtaining permits and public pressure against nuclear energy expansion.

As new plants open there is a need for operating personnel. Around 13 special types of engineers are needed to run a plant including easily recognized fields such as electrical, mechanical, chemical, and civil. It also includes new specialists such as nuclear, systems, ceramic, human factors, materials, reactor safety, standards development, reactor, and project engineers.

There are many jobs for technicians which didn't exist twenty years ago. They include nuclear power plant inspectors, nuclear fuels specialists, quality assurance specialists, fabrication of fuel assemblers, instrument servicepersons, and systems reliability analysts. There are jobs for those trained in the life sciences as health physicists and environmental specialists. Physical scientists needed include chemists, soil and air specialists, radio chemists and geochemists.

Those who choose to go into atomic power are in an excellent position to move into the new fusion energy plants when they are more fully developed early in the 21st century.

Nuclear Fusion

The theory of fusion energy has become familiar to most of us since the development of the first hydrogen bomb. If you heat hydrogen atoms to an unimaginably high temperature, and confine them in some way, they become frantically active, run into one another, and some of them fuse. Tremendous amounts of energy are released when this fusion takes place. Fusion is no longer just a theoretical possibility applicable to only a single explosion. It is more like an engineering problem.

The problems of confining the atoms and heating them to such a high temperature that a continuous power flow can take place, have not been solved. The Russians came up with the right shape for a strong magnetic field in which the hydrogen atoms can be contained and heated. There is no known substance which could be heated to a high enough temperature. Americans have made many improvements in this device named by the Russians, a tokamak.

The Magnetic Fusion Energy Engineering Act of 1980 committed the U.S. to spend 20 billion dollars before the end of the century. A much-refined and enlarged tokamak now under development is a test facility intended to show by 1990 whether this approach is economically feasible. There are at least two other approaches to solving the engineering problems being researched at present.

In a brief energy article in *National Geographic*, only one column was devoted to "The Fusion Solution."[1] It summed up the problems and the hopes. "Fusion offers immense advantages over today's fission reactors; only a fraction of the radioactivity, no threat of meltdown, and a plentiful source of duteriom from water. But fusion technology is so complex that some feel it will never be inexpensive enough to use. In any case, commercial fusion will not come before the year 2000." Other experts would place that date even further into the future. An opinion given in *Forbes* magazine is that, "In the long run, there can be no doubt that fusion, using cheap and plentiful sources for the energy it produces, will prove both economic and desirable."[2]

It will be many years before the fusion industry employs many people. Meanwhile, in the research laboratories like Princeton's Plasma Physics Laboratory, there would seem to be a constant shortage of super PhD's trained in plasma physics.

---

[1] "A Status Report on Energy," *National Geographic Magazine*, February 1981, p. 83.
[2] Seneker, Harold: "Clean and Plentiful Energy on the Way," *Forbes*, November 24, 1980, p. 38.

Jobs With A Future

Biochemist
Chemist
Economic analyst
Environmental specialist
Fusion engineer
Hazardous waste management technician
Health physicist
Nuclear fuels specialist
Nuclear instrument serviceperson
Nuclear power plant operator

Nuclear quality assessment inspector
Nuclear reactor manager
Nuclear reactor operator
Nuclear reactor technician
Nuclear specialist
Nuclear waste manager
Out of core fuel manager
Quantitative risk assessment analyst
Radiation physicist
Radio chemist

For Further Information—Some starting points

American Nuclear Energy Council, 1750 K Street, N.W., Suite 300, Washington, D.C. 20006, (202) 296-4520.

American Nuclear Society, 555 N. Kensington Park, LaGrange Park, Illinois 60525, (203) 677-7305. The Society publishes a very useful list of schools which offer educational programs in nuclear energy.

Americans for Nuclear Energy, P.O. Box 28371, Washington, D.C. 20005, (703) 241-2007.

Bennett, Donald. *The Elements of Nuclear Energy.* New York: Longmans Inc., 1981.

Energy and Jobs for the 80's. The National Coalition, 1201 Connecticut Avenue, N.W., Washington, D.C. 20036, (202) 331-2400. $5.00.

Federation of American Scientists, 307 Massachusetts Avenue, N.E., Washington, D.C. 20002, (202) 546-3300.

Fermoselle, Rafel. *Energy Occupations in Demand,* R. F. Associates, P.O. Box 5575, Arlington, Virginia, 1980. (Out of print.)

Greenhalgh, G. *The Necessity of Nuclear Power.* New York: State Mutual Books and Periodical Service, 1980.

Mann, Martin. *Peacetime Uses of Atomic Energy.* New York: Thomas Y. Crowell, 1975.

Nuclear Energy Women, 7101 Wisconsin Avenue, Washington, D.C. 20014, (301) 654-9280.

Oil, Chemical, and Atomic Workers International Union, P.O. Box 2812, Denver, Colorado 80201, (303) 893-0811.

The Outlook for Nuclear Power. National Academy Press, 2101 Constitution Avenue, N.W., Washington, D.C. 20418, 1980.

Williams, N. and R. Sher (editors). *Progress in Nuclear Energy*. Elmsford, N.Y.: Pergamon Press, 1979.

Chapter 6

ENERGY INDUSTRY CAREERS: SOLAR, HYDRO, AND GEOTHERMAL

All the energy the human race has ever used since the beginning, what we are using now, and what we shall use in the future comes from the sun. The sun grew the forests which fueled the world's first camp and cooking fires. The sun grew the trees and swamps which later were buried, compressed, and became the coal, oil, and natural gas we depend on. The sun draws up water into the clouds. When it rains and runs down hill, it provides the water power to turn the turbines in hydro-electric plants.

Hydro-Electric

Water power has been used to turn mill wheels since the 16th century and to generate electricity since it was discovered in the 19th century. It supplies slightly more than 4% of America's energy needs. It scarcely rates a line in a section on "The Newest of the New" except to mention that it is being rediscovered. Federal officials estimate that there are 5,000 dam sites where small hydro-electric plants could be built. Many small hydro-electric plants, which once served small towns were abandoned when the vast projects like TVA and Hoover Dam were built. Many are now being restored and what they produce is fed into the power grid for the region.

Two examples of this new interest may be cited. In Maine, the Franklin County Energy Project received a small grant from the U.S. Department of Energy to consult with energy committees in any of the 26 towns in its county. The project will assess the potential for building hydro facilities, as well as on the options for use of wind, solar, or biomass power.

In Tennessee, citizens formed the Lincoln County Energy Conservation Committee. It is investigating all possibilities for improving the county's energy situation including renovating the hydropower facility at the Harm's Dam, the original source of the county's electricity.

The total power potential from existing small dams and undeveloped small dam sites is estimated at 200 million killowatts or about 40% of the nation's need.

Photovoltaic Cells

The world first became aware of photovoltaic cells during the space explorations. We learned that the Space Lab had banks of these cells which could transfer radiant energy of the sun into electricity needed in the lab. These cells are solid state devices which utilize the photo-electronic properties of the semi-conductors. Silicon crystals, the most commonly used semi-conductor, are grown in the laboratory then sliced wafer thin. These are the same silicon crystals which led to dramatic developments in computers and electronics. Despite the fact that silicon is a cheap and widely available element, the process of growing silicon crystals in a laboratory is time consuming and expensive. Now that the cells are being manufactured commercially, the price is steadily dropping. At the same time, the cost of generating electricity by conventional means is rising. Many energy specialists believe these two cost curves will cross sometime in this decade. As photovoltaics become competitive with other power systems, the market for them will explode. Once installed, they cost nothing to operate.

Photovoltaic electrical systems are already in use in a number of experimental homes. The electricity produced during hours of sunlight is often in excess of that needed to operate the machinery in the household. This excess can be fed into the utility company's power grid and a special system of metering makes certain that a credit is given on the utility bill. Since the cells only operate during the day, the utility company is used for electricity at night—at least until some one discovers a way to store the excess.

Art Litka of the Kennedy Space Center in Cape Canaveral, Florida, who lives in one of the experimental houses, estimates that by the end of the 1980s people will be able to generate from their own sources up to 75% of their household electricity needs.

Photovoltaics are producing electricity for almost every other electrical need as well. Some were cited in *Shining Examples*.[1] The

---

[1] *Shining Examples*, Center for Renewable Resources, 1001 Connecticut Avenue, N.W., Washington, D.C. 20036, 1980.

Cameron Farm Project (Cameron, Arizona), a community project for the construction of a solar greenhouse complex, uses photovoltaic cells for its electrical needs.

In the Indian village of Schuchuli, Arizona, which formerly depended on kerosene lamps, an array of 192 photovoltaic cells provides sufficient electricity to power 14 refrigerator-freezers, a washing machine, a sewing machine, the village water pump, lights for the village's 15 homes, a church, and a feast house. A photovoltaic signal system sponsored and funded by Southern Railway is located at the railroad crossing of the Bombigbee River near Jackson, Alabama. The photovoltaic array controls signals and circuits for the drawbridge crossing. The Lea County Electric Co-op in New Mexico is sponsoring a 150 kilowatt photovoltaic system which will span three to four acres and provide 30 to 50 percent of the power needs for a shopping center.

The infant solar cell industry is growing very fast. As an illustration, the Solarex Corporation, the world's largest manufacturer of photovoltaic solar cells, is less than 10 years old. Its new six million dollar showcase plant in Frederick, Maryland, will further boost output. Both American and German manufacturers are coming out with less expensive solar cells.

Biomass

This is the burning of organic waste products, garbage or anything else combustible. The heat converts water into steam to turn the turbines of a generator. Biomass is particularly exciting because it has the potential of solving two major urban problems; providing enough electricity and disposing of garbage.

In 1978, New York City collected some 21,500 tons of garbage daily. Landfills were becoming scarce and located further and further from the city. Towing garbage by barge out into the ocean and dumping it was being frowned upon, and still the problem grew. New York's garbage has a relatively high concentration of dry paper and plastic which means its usable energy content may be considerably higher than in other cities where moist organic material makes up a larger portion. In Tokyo, for example, an estimated 30% of the garbage by weight is water. Burning this "high quality garbage" can turn electric generators as well as any other fuel.

A early initiative to develop a biomass program for New York City began in 1948. The plan was to locate new waste conversion plants in a series of new industrial parks planned for the New York and New

Jersey areas. The power could then be sold to the industrial occupants of the parks. These plans met with resistance almost from the start, and little has developed from the idea. Although the new industrial parks are still planned, the conversion plants will not be built in or even near them.

The technology for turning garbage into electricity has been used in Europe for more than 20 years. Only about six of some 265 waste-conversion plants in the world are located in the United States. Given the increasing problems of garbage disposal and power shortages, such plants are bound to increase in the U.S. providing some way can be found to deal with complaining groups. Consolidated Edison of New York offered, as long ago as 1965, to build such a plant, but neighborhood groups keep saying, "Put it somewhere else."

The concept of biomass also includes the use of organic materials (waste or otherwise) to produce other fuels as well as steam power. This has usually been done using a fermentation process—a still, as explained in the section on synfuels. Heat may be recovered more directly, however, through the use of "digestors." A large greenhouse in Memphis, Tennessee, uses what it calls a "solganic" greenhouse. In addition, to direct solar heat, back-up heat is provided by composting 5,400 cubic feet of sawdust. This is loaded into bins in the fall. A feeder pipe drips a mixture of water and nitrogen on each pile to moisten it. Small fans force air through to aerate the mixture where it picks up heat. The warmed air is then blown into the greenhouse. Over the winter about 30% of total possible energy contained in the sawdust is released. In spring, the remainder is sold as a substitute for peat moss.

The Buo-Gas Company of Colorado is a leader in bioconversion technology. It concerns itself with the feasibility of applying bioconversion technology to small and large farms, ranches, feedlots, hog farms, chicken farms, race tracks, municipal sewage plants, and power plants. It conducts laboratory experiments to determine the power yield coefficient of different manures.

Wind

Sixty years ago, America's farmland was dotted with windmills. They were used to pump water and run generators which provided electricity for use on the farm. When Rural Electrification brought power lines to farmers, they began to buy electricity to power their pumps. Windmills fell into disuse.

The inventor and manufacture of the Jacobs Wind Plant went out of business in 1960. Now 77, Marcellus Jacobs has come back from Florida to re-open a factory near Minneapolis to turn out 10-kilowatt wind plants, each capable of producing enough electricity to keep all the electric gadgets and appliances humming in an average home (2,000 kilowatt hours a month). They carry a current price tag of $10,000. The Jacobs windmills are a far cry from the lazy, four-bladed windmills which decorate so much delft pottery. They look like a three-bladed airplane propeller with a slim helicopter tail, mounted on a tall metal tower.

Beside small wind plants ideally suited for rural homes, Washington is encouraging larger ones for use by towns or rural electric co-operatives. A wind power plant in Clayton, N.M., produces enough energy to meet the power requirements of one-sixth of the town's 3,000 residents. In Boone, N.C., one is mounted on a 150-foot tower. It has a 200 foot rotor and will produce power for more than 300 homes. These larger machines have only two slender blades on their rotors.

Meanwhile, the Grumman Aerospace Corporation is experimenting with building the yen machine (named for the inventor). It looks more like a grain elevator than a windmill. The device located inside an enormous tower will whip wind into controlled vortex—a tornado. This creates a vacuum at the bottom and multiplies the force of the air driving a turbine.

The Japanese have built a prototype of what may become a new fleet of sail-aided cargo ships. In a 30-knot wind abcam, the sails on the fully-loaded ship can provide 53% of the power to travel at 12 knots. A microcomputer system is programmed to give commands to trim the steel-framed canvas sails by rotating the masts. Fuel savings have been shown to be as high as 50%—an important factor for oil-starved Japan.

Several other kinds of wind assisted ships are on the drawing boards or being built. Some make use of wind turbines. Others have "sails" resembling airplane wings fixed upright on the deck. A 1981 issue of *Quest* magazine pictured more than a dozen designs.

The Wind Energy Systems Act of 1980 initiated an eight-year, 900 million dollar program to develop cost-effective wind power systems in the U.S. Clearly we no longer feel that the windmill is obsolete, but will continue to develop it. It is estimated that 30,000 large turbines and thousands of small ones could supply 10% of our nation's needs by the year 2000.

Geothermal

Some lucky residents of our Northwest, Iceland, and other places, have for years had geothermal (hot water) heat circulated through their homes at little or no cost. Around 70 percent of new homes in Iceland use geothermal heat. The United States has one of the world's biggest geothermal fields—the Geysers in Northern California. Steam harnessed there has generating capacity of 608 megawatts, and ultimately will hit 2,000 megawatts. In all, 37 states have some geothermal resources.

For many years scientists, geologists and volcanologists have been trying to determine ways to tap the tremendous and inexhaustable heat resources stored in the earth. No one who witnessed the awesome force of Mt. St. Helena in 1979 and 1980 can doubt that the molten core of the earth contains all the energy we will ever need. Controlling it, putting it under our control so it can be of practical use is still in the experimental stage. Federal funds are helping companies and local governments, mainly in the West, to locate new geothermal wells. Geothermal energy is now used for space and hot water heating for a hospital in Marin, Texas; for a food processing plant in Madison County, Idaho; for space heating in Boise, Idaho; for heat to dry grain at a ranch in Rapid City, S.D.; and for space heating for 14 office buildings in Klamath Falls, Oregon.

Most of the research in the area of magma energy studies has been directed by Sandia Laboratories, a private facility in Albuquerque, New Mexico.[1] At present, Sandia is involved in a project for the U.S. Government and involves scientists from universities, the U.S. Geological Survey, and the National Magma Energy Advisory Panel. The panel consists of experts in volcanology, geophysics, magma petrology, geochemistry, and materials sciences. They regularly review the project's research.

Ocean Thermal

The natural proclivities of cold water to sink to the bottom and warm water to rise to the top (convection currents) can be used to generate electricity. It is particularly true in tropical areas where the

---

[1] A magma is a pocket of molten rock which begins to move toward the surface of the earth from the upper mantle (some 400 miles down) where the temperature is 2,300° F. Parts of the magma pool may move through the inner and sometimes the outer crust of the Earth by melting the rocks immediately above it. Magmas are the source of heat for geothermal springs and volcanos.

deep ocean water temperatures are often 37 degrees or more colder than the surface water. Ocean thermal energy conversion uses the warm surface water to heat a liquid refrigerant and convert it to vapor. In this form it drives a turbine. Cold water from the depths is then pumped in to convert the refrigerant to it's original liquid form. The circular process is kept going continuously.

One government funded project is being carried out in Hawaii. It will probably be the early 1990s before this will be commercially feasible, such as creating electricity for small islands.

Solar Salt Ponds

This new method of power generation is being developed by the Israelis. It uses solar heated, salt water to turn specially designed turbines to produce electricity. Since salt water is heavier than fresh water, it sinks to the bottom of the pond. A thin layer of fresh water always covers the top, providing the water remains calm and undisturbed.

Salt water also absorbs heat more rapidly than fresh water. The Israeli research pond at Ein Bokken on the Dead Sea covers 70,000 square feet and is the largest one in existence. Here brine heated by the sun a few feet below the surface can reach temperatures near boiling. Pipes take the hot brine from near the bottom of the pond to an evaporator. Rising steam turns a turbine on its way to a condensor tank.

Salt does not vaporize. Although it goes into solution in water, what condenses is fresh water. This is returned to the top layer of the salt pond. Most amateur cooks have inadvertently proved this principle for themselves by allowing a pan of salted water to boil dry. The salt remains on the bottom of the pan. In working salt ponds, the production of salt is a useful by-product.

Several locations in the United States are appropriate for the use of this method. Since 1979, the largest salt pond in the U.S. (21,000 square feet) has been operating in the city of Miamisburg, Ohio. It cost $70,000 to develop and produces electricity at 1.8 cents per kilowatt hour to heat water in a swimming pool and space in a recreation building.

The Jet Propulsion Laboratory is developing plans for what could become a 6,000 megawatt generating complex on the Salton Sea in California. In Utah, approval is pending on a $1.2 million appropriation from Congress to do the same thing on Salt Lake. This method of generating power also helps reduce the salinity of water where that is a problem, such as in the Colorado River and the Salton Sea.

Direct Solar Collectors

Collectors can also be used to generate heat for steam to turn a turbine. A pilot project in Crosbyton, Texas uses a solar-fossil fuel hybrid electric power plant which will be operated by the existing rural electric co-op in the area. One of a proposed ten 200-foot fixed, hemispherical bowl collectors is already in operation in Crosbyton. When the other solar collectors are built, they will provide 20% of the needed power for the area. The new fossil fuel plant will provide 80%. Using solar energy in this way will reduce the cost of fossil fuel needed by 20%.

Cogeneration

Cogeneration is not a separate method of generating power. It is a concept which applies to all energy facilities which generate power by more than one method. The Crosbyton, Texas system described above is an example of cogeneration. Many of the new facilities make use of more than one method. Most buildings which utilize passive solar heating also use energy provided by other methods—usually natural gas, oil, or electricity. But many projects also use entirely new methods. A farm in Michigan, for example, generates electricity from manure produced by 350 head of cattle. The manure is processed into methane, which powers an internal combustion engine that runs an electric generator.

Some conventional methods of generating power produce an excess of hot water. This frequently becomes a problem in the streams into which it is discharged. One project uses some of the hot water for aquaculture—to grow a sizable crop of fish. Power plant designs must be modified in order to make this type of use possible, and that is already being done in Europe. It is now being considered by power companies in this country as they plan new facilities.

The Job Outlook:

Much thought and creative inguinity has gone into developing alternative sources of energy in the past decade. This was spurred on by the rising cost of oil and more importantly by the stark fact that oil resources of the world are diminishing at such a rapid rate that oil cannot continue to be our major source of supplying heat and transportation much beyond the year 2000.

The different projects described in this chapter are largely experimental. Those interested in riding the solar energy wave into the future should prepare themselves by keeping up with what is going on—studying actual applications such as those described in Chapter 7. This new branch of the energy industry does not yet employ many workers. Opportunities may be found to get acquainted with a project or procedure, by finding a full-time, part time or volunteer job with the project—even on a business or clerical level, if you have no applicable skills. This enables you to see what is developing and to learn what additional steps in education and preparation may be needed. The Reagan administration cut funding for some of these projects or turned them over to local communities, so some persistent research may be required to find the project or projects that are right for you.

Natural resources are going to have to provide the ultimate answer to our world-wide energy problem. It is only in the last 100 years that the human race met any of its energy means by using petroleum. For thousands of years before that, other sources were used ranging from wood to whale oil, from charcoal to peat, and even olive oil. There was heavy reliance on human and animal muscle power.

As society became more complex we tended to selected the energy source that was cheapest and easiest to exploit. Animal power began to be replaced by water power in the 16th, 17th and 18th centuries. In the 19th century, coal with some assistance from natural gas and oil powered the Industrial Revolution. Once we discovered electricity, we found a whole range of natural resources could be exploited to produce electricity—a cleaner and more versatile fuel than we ever had before. In the 20th century, instead of coal, we began to use oil to make electricity as well as to make fuel for our growing number of machines used on farms, in factories and in transportation. By the time the modern energy industry got under way in the 1970s, we had narrowed our choice of natural resources to an extremely heavy reliance on oil.

The late comedian and philosopher Will Rogers, advised his listeners to "buy land, as the Good Lord had stopped making any more of it." In the same vein, the longer range solutions to our energy problems, and the clue to careers of the future in this area, will involve a movement toward utilizing a wider variety of natural resources. Ways to exploit simple things such as the fact that the wind blows, the tides rise and fall, salt water more readily absorbs heat, and the core of the earth is composed of volatile, extremely hot substances, are already being used experimentally. All projects make use of the latest in new and emerging technologies.

The process of increasing our reliance upon a wider variety of different resources will require major changes in lifestyle. Can we learn to cope with such problems as the bulk required for a wind mill or (as described in the next chapter) the equipment needed for a solar power system. Certainly, it is much simpler to call up the power company and order electricity or gas delivered—to be paid for monthly, than to face the problems and initial heavy expense required when using more natural power sources.

The Oil Embargo of the early 1970s called for the first of these major adjustments in our way of doing things. As the price of gasoline at the retail gas station rose from 28–33 cents per gallon in the early 1960s, to over $1.40 in the late 1970s, many jumped on the bandwagon to develop new energy sources. But too many quietly slipped off the wagon when gasoline prices began to fall in the early 1980s. At the present time there is little public pressure to move ahead with alternate energy sources, as the Government cut back on grant money, many of the industries and communities cut back or eliminated their alternate energy projects. Yet futurists agree that oil resources will not last far beyond the early years of the 21st century. We have little more than 20 years to accomplish the changeover. Whether we make it or not depends upon making a much stronger national and personal commitment to it.

If you are interested in planning for a career in the newly emerging energy areas, keep in mind that not all the new jobs are on the PhD or even professional level. Technicians are needed in all areas, as well as persons with traditional skills which can be adapted for use in one of these new fields.

Note: Resources relating to solar energy appear at the end of Chapter 7.

Chapter 7

ENERGY INDUSTRY CAREERS: SOLAR HEATING, COOLING, CONSERVATION, AND ENVIRONMENTAL PROTECTION

Solar Heating and Cooling

A *New Yorker* cartoon shows a man and a woman in conversation at a crowded cocktail party. "I can never remember," the woman says, "are you fully woodburning, or are you just supplementary solar?"

One good result of the severe oil shortage in 1974 was to start our thinking about conserving energy. An immediate result was a boom in the technologies of solar heating and cooling. Solar houses began to spring up, not just in the Southwest but every latitude as the problems of insulating homes to conserve heat, and of using the heat of the sun began to be explored in earnest. Hundreds of single, experimental homes were built and the technology continued to improve. Just recently a few developers in the Southwest have begun solar homes developments, applying mass production techniques to this area.

There are seven basic types of solar home, and while each type requires persons with the traditional building trade skills, there is also a need for new kinds of specialists. Some of those with the new specialties have added them to skills they already possessed. This has increased the number of jobs open to them.

1. The first type uses direct, passive solar heating. These houses are characterized by large areas of glass on their South side. In this country, however, direct, passive, solar heated homes usually require supplementary conventional heating systems for use on cloudy days. The occupants also may lose some of their day time privacy behind their walls of glass. The glass walls also require expensive, insulated drapes which can be drawn to preserve the heat on winter nights.

2. A second kind of solar house is based on the principle of indirect, passive solar gain. A trombe masonry wall, or a wall of water contained in opaque or transparent plastics, is placed several feet behind the wall of glass. This captures and stores much of the heat which streams in during the day. Floors near the glass wall also are generally constructed of heat-absorbing tile or slate. However, trombe masonry walls do block the light, while contained water walls block the view. This type of house also may need a back-up heating system.

3. Super-insulated houses, usually with limited windows are classified as solar homes. Whole new standards for insulation have been developed to make a house as air-tight as possible. Super-insulated homes have great cost-effectiveness, but they do have some disadvantages. A build-up of odors, humidity, and noxious combustion products may occur. Most existing houses can be turned into super-insulated homes. In addition to dramatic savings on heating bills, the owners may also claim a tax credit for insulating their homes.

4. Houses with rooftop collectors have active solar heating systems. Collectors can collect either hot water or hot air. Those which heat air generally depend on natural convection currents (hot air rises—cold air falls) to help distribute the heat around the house. Heat can be stored in large bins of rocks in the basement over which the hot air has traveled. Systems which heat water generally have complicated systems of copper pipes which may occasionally require plumbing service. Excess hot water can be stored in large tanks in the basement and the heat it provides can be used in the evenings or on cloudy days.

The word "active" comes from the need for pumps and fans to distribute the heated water or air to where it is needed or stored. These systems also need back-up or supplementary heating which may vary from conventional gas or oil furnaces to wood fire places, coal stoves or electric heat pumps.

5. The double-envelope passive solar system is based on building certain key walls double. This takes advantage of the natural convection currents of heated and cold air. A controversy is going on over whether the additional expense of building the double wall is, or is not greater than the cost and heat this method saves. Like the others, a back-up heating system is required.

6. The underground or earth-sheltered house is another way to save heat while at the same time blending the house into the landscape. Usually the North side and the roof are buried under, or covered with, a thick layer of earth. Much of the West and East sides

may also be covered. The South is left open to the sun. The earth covering moderates temperatures, deadens noise, and almost eliminates exterior maintenance. Improperly designed or built underground houses may develop severe humidity problems. Costs for building are generally a little higher than for conventionally built, energy efficient houses.

7. Several photovoltaic-powered, direct gain heating systems have been developed, but they are, as yet, prohibitively expensive. However, by 1986 electric rates nationally are expected to double. Photovoltaic systems may be available then for less than $15,000 and may be able to deliver electricity competitively. Several experimental homes already use banks of solar cells to provide a small percentage of their electricity needs. One is described later.

There are more than 50,000 solar-heated homes in the U.S. using one or more of the above types, and the industry is growing.

Solar Hot Water Heating

Most homes utilizing solar heat also install a solar hot water system. These systems can also be installed in existing non-solar heated homes. In fact, under the Carter Administration, the White House had solar collectors installed on the roof to aid in heating its hot water.

Solar Cooling or Air Conditioning

Must less has been said, and presumably done, about cooling systems which utilize non-conventional means. One method commonly employed in new, energy-efficient homes, is cooling tubes or pipes. This system uses pipes buried in the ground beneath the frost level either under the house or in the yard. The constant temperature of the ground at this level is 52°F. When air or a liquid is pumped through these pipes, it absorbs the temperature of the surrounding earth. When this is pumped back into the house, which has a temperature, say, of 90°F, the cool air or liquid lowers the temperature of the house and eventually becomes the same temperature as the room. The liquid or air is then pumped into the ground, and the whole circular process continues.

In winter when the prevailing temperature outdoors may be considerably below 52°, the process can be reversed. The air or liquid which has absorbed the earth's temperature may then be made to give up this heat, to be added to the supply for the house.

The standard heat pump, now being installed in so many new homes, works on a principle similar to that of the air conditioner. It uses a refrigerant or heat exchanger to pick up the unwanted heat in the air of a house. This is then pumped outside. The difference is that in a heat pump, the cycle can be reversed in the winter. Even at 28 or 30 degrees, the pump's heat exchanging liquid can pick up heat from the outside, air, condense it, and deliver it as additional warmth for the inside of the house. In mild climates, direct solar gain houses with heat pumps will need the assistance of back-up systems only during exceptional cold snaps, or long periods of cloudiness.

Solariums and Greenhouses

These are often an integral part of the heating systems for solar homes. They are often located between the glass wall and the trombe wall and contribute to heating as well as interior decoration. Some people grow their winter vegetables in them. Others set up a solar hot tub area.

A Hybrid Example

At this stage in the development of solar energy technology, none of the seven types of housing described above relies only on one system. Generally, they combine several. Fortunately the computer industry has come up with the home computer which makes it possible to manage all these complex options. Individual functions needing management include opening and closing shutters or vents when certain temperatures are reached, turning on or off pumps or fans to assist in the circulation of solar heated air or water, and opening or closing blinds or insulated drapes when the sun goes up or down.

A large Connecticut residence (5,300 square feet) makes use of three energy systems, all managed by an Apple Computer. Mechanically assisted active solar systems meets 45% of the home's heat and hot water needs. A 1,000 gallon water tank stores the heat collected by two arrays of flat plate copper collectors. Heat for space heating is distributed by fans forcing air past a network of pipes containing warmed water. The floors of poured concrete, over insulated foam and paved with slate, radiate heat absorbed from the sun.

All the fans and controls for the active solar system are powered by 150 square feet of photovoltaic cells which meet 5% of the electrical needs of the house. Two separate, 65 gallon tanks hold a solar pre-heated domestic hot water supply. An electric heat pump provides a space heating back-up.

An additional 15% of the heating needs come from non-mechanical, passive solar sources. The house is partially buried on the North side. It has maximum exposure to the sunny South. A greenhouse amplifies direct solar gain, storing heat in an eight-inch thick concrete floor. Two energy zones are arranged so separate solar and back-up systems can work independently or in tandem as needed. The computer quite literally makes it possible to take full advantage of all these natural sources of heat. Should a householder have to control all these systems manually, he or she would spend hours just turning switches on and off, closing and opening shutters, etc.

The Solar Jobs Outlook:

At this time the greatest personnel needs are for highly trained scientists and engineers. However, there are increasingly opportunities for pipefitters-welders, sheet metal workers, plumbers, and carpenters.

"It seems more likely that jobs in solar energy will go to workers who are now employed in traditional oil, gas, and electric heating and air conditioning. They are either being retrained or plans are being prepared to retrain them," says *Energy Occupations in Demand*. The sheet metal industry gives a course in installing solar equipment to about three hundred apprentice teachers. Other apprenticeship programs will likely offer similar training.

According to the Solar Energy Research Institute, 600 post-secondary institutions target one or more courses in solar energy in a recent school year and more than 135 offered programs leading to a degree. Approximately 300 people teach courses in solar energy, most at vocational-technical schools and community colleges. This picture changes rapidly, so if the solar energy field is of interest to you, you need to scout around to discover what training is available in your location.

In an industry so new, it is often possible to start at the bottom and gain on-the-job training as you move up. More and more manufacturers are entering the field and many find it necessary to train their own workers. If you already have skills in one of the more standard trades mentioned above, using them in the solar industry is a good way to move from a field which may be diminishing to an expanding one. According to a Department of Energy report, about 22,500 people were employed in jobs relating to solar energy in 1970. There are probably twice that number today, since the same report estimated that that number was expected to triple by 1983.

Conservation and Environmental Protection

"I'm in sanitation now, you know," announces an immaculately white clad comedian, Jonathan Winters, in a television commercial for plastic trash bags. The change from "garbage man" to "sanitation worker" is much more than a name change. More and more we are linking up waste disposal jobs with recycling and energy retrieval methods. We see them as a part of environmental protection.

The Environmental Protection Careers Guidebook, published by the U.S. Department of Labor, lists more than 100 occupations. Many of them did not exist a decade ago. Conservation and environmental protection do overlap, and both contribute to our interest in preserving the good condition of the earth for future generations.

As the oil shortage increased, and prices of all kinds of energy soared, the only response most of us could make was to conserve—to use less. Government campaigns encouraged insulation of homes to use less energy. The media was rife with reports of how many million barrels of oil were left in the world's underground reservoirs, and how long they would last. The happy-go-lucky days of cheap power were over, we were told, and many economists projected gloomy pictures of the future.

Alternative energy sources began to be developed immediately, but they remained very expensive—that is, more expensive than oil at its then existing price. Conservation continues to make sense both for the individual and for the nation. Insulation and other heat conservation techniques will lower the cost of energy no matter what source of energy is used.

But there is an additional reason for our interest in conservation. Much has been done in the past 15 years to preserve and improve the quality of our air and water. This has been done through public pressure groups, legislation, and programs mandated by the legislation. One example is the legislation which led to the curtailment of factory smoke stack emissions—a leading cause of acid rain. Environmental protection is becoming even more important as we begin to exploit our vast resources of coal and oil shales.

Since most of the new professionals and technicians who will work in conservation or environmental protection, will be employed by state, city or local governments, their jobs will be discussed in more detail in a future book in this series covering the burgeoning service industry.

The Energy Jobs Picture as a Whole:

The energy industry as a whole is on the move. Some of its many and diverse parts are scarcely out of or still in the research, pilot project or experimental stages. Other parts of the energy industry are manufacturing and distributing new more efficient systems. As a nation, we have clearly moved away from our original dependance upon one or two sources of energy. We no longer are intent on developing monolithic electric power systems. We are beginning to make more creative use of the many different ways there are of generating electricity. Most futurists think this will make us a stronger nation as the various sections of the country will be more independent in regard to their power needs.

For young persons on the threshold of careers, or for older persons who need to make career changes, opportunities are developing in many aspects of the energy industry.

The Job Picture:

New publications are coming out daily. In an industry which is growing and changing so rapidly, one needs to cover many of them just to keep a running tab on the situation. There are needs in the solar energy industry for persons with old-fashioned trades, for electricians, pipe-fitters, plumbers, carpenters and those with other building trade skills. There is room for persons with every degree of specialized education in those aspects which are still more engaged in research and development. Acquired skills may need to be refurbished and up-dated, and often a person needs to move to a different part of the country before he or she can apply skills in a new and emerging industry.

Opportunities are somewhat curtailed right now (in the early 1980s) by the recession in the housing industry. This is temporary and if anything, it has caused a pent-up need for housing in America which will improve for the need for workers who know how to build the latest, energy-efficient houses.

Jobs With A Future

Active solar systems equipment installer (carpenter, electrician, plumber)
Environmental engineer
Environmental health scientist
Environmental protection professional
Hazardous waste manager
HVAC mechanic
Rango manager
Reclamation technologist
Solar energy modular assembler
Solar energy research scientist
Solar energy systems designer
Solar energy technician
Silicon production technician
Waste technician
Water specialist
Water pollution specialist

Persons in the following careers may work in more than one branch of the energy industry

Alternate energy technologist   Energy efficiency technician
Energy consultant   Energy manager

For Further Information—Some starting points

Conservation Directory, 1981, 26th edition, National Wildlife Federation, 1412 Sixteenth Street, N.W., Washington, D.C. 20036, (202) 797-6800.

Deudney, Daniel, *Rivers of Energy: The Hydropower Potential*, Worldwatch Paper 44, June 1981, Worldwatch Institute, 1776 Massachusetts Avenue, N.W., Washington, D.C. 20036.

Ecology and Your Career, U.S. Department of Labor, Bureau of Labor Statistics. Reprints available at 50¢ each from any Regional Office of the Bureau of Labor Statistics, U.S. Department of Human Services. Consult phone book.

Energy and Architecture: The Solar and Conservation Potential, Worldwatch Institute, 1776 Massachusetts Avenue, N.W., Washington, D.C. 20036. $2.00.

Energy and Jobs for the 80s, The National Urban Coalition, 1201 Connecticut Avenue, N.W., Washington, D.C. 20036, (202) 331-2400. $5.00.

Energy Occupations Handbook, New Jersey Vocational-Technical Curriculum Laboratory, 4103 Kilmer Campus, Rutgers—The State University of New Jersey, New Brunswick, New Jersey 08903, 1979, Paperback $7.00.

Energy Related Careers. ERIC Document Reproduction Service, P.O. Box 190, Arlington, Virginia 22210. $3.65 plus $1.40 for postage and handling.

Environmental Protection Careers Guidebook, U.S. Department of Labor, Employment and Training Administration and U.S. Environmental Protection Agency. (See above to locate a copy or it may be in libraries.)

Ericson, Katherine, *The Solar Jobs Book*, Brick House Book Publishers, 3 Main Street, Andover, Massachusetts 01801, Paperback, 1980.

Fermoselle, Rafael, *Energy Occupations in Demand*, R. F. Associates, P.O. Box 5572, Arlington, Virginia 22305, 1980. (Out of print.)

Gottlieb, Richard and Sandra Oddo (editors). *The Solar Energy Directory*. New York: H. W. Wilson Company, 1980. This book costs $50 but should be available in larger libraries. It lists manufacturers, associations, governmental agencies, training centers, and information sources in solar energy.

Hunt, V. Daniel. *Solar Energy Dictionary*. New York: Industrial Press, Inc., 1981.

International Solar Energy Society—American Section; A.T.U., Box 1416, Kileen, Texas 76541, (817) 526-1300. Publishes magazine, *Solar Age*. Subscription $20.00 per year.

Manpower in Energy-Related Activities—A Summary and Review of Recent Studies, 1982 (developed by the U.S. Department of Energy). Available at a fee through the National Technical Information Service, U.S. Department of Commerce, Springfield, Virginia 22161.

Martindale, David, *Earth Shelters*. New York: E. P. Dutton, 1981, paperback.

Maycock, Paul D., and Stirewalt, Edward H., *Photovoltacis: Sunlight to Electricity In One Step*, Brick House Publishers, 1981, Andover, Massachusetts.

Millard, Reed, *Solar Energy for Tomorrow's World*. New York: Julian Messmer.

National Solar Energy Education Directory. Washington, Superintendent of Documents, U.S. Government Printing Office, 1982. (Stock Number 061-00-00368) $5.50. Cites solar energy courses, programs, and curricula at 750 colleges and universities as a guide to student planning careers in this area.

Parr, Jack, *The Wind Power Book*. Palo Alto, California: Cheshire Books, 1981. $11.95 (U.S.A.). A complete and usable compilation of information on selecting, building and using wind power systems for pumping and/or generating.

Solar Energy Buyer's Guide and Directory. Solar Data, 13 Evergreen Road, Hampton, New Hampshire 03843, (603) 926-8082. $20.00. Lists over 3000 companies in the United States active in solar heating and cooling, solar electricity, bioconversion, and wind and ocean thermal conversion.

Solar Energy Industry Association, Inc., Suite 800, 1001 Connecticut Avenue, N.W., Washington, D.C. 20036, (202) 293-1000. Publishes association monthly newsletter—*SEIA News*.

Solar Energy Information Locator, 1978, Energy Research Institute, 1536 Cole Blvd., Golden, Colorado 80401. Free. Note: This small booklet was prepared for the Solar Energy Information Data Bank. It was developed by the Institute. It gives addresses, phone numbers, areas of interest publications, and information services for organizations and government agencies.

Solar Energy Institute of North America, 1110 Sixth Street, N.W., Washington, D.C. 20001, (202) 298-4411.

McKay, Murphy G., *Energy Management*, Butterworth & Co., 10 Tower Office Park, Woburn, Massachusetts 01801, 1982.

Hedley, Don, *World Energy, The Facts and The Future*, Facts on File, Inc., 119 W. 57th Street, New York, New York 10019, 1981.

Solar Energy Source Book, an 800-page paperback listing of manufacturers, and businesses involved in the solar energy field. $15.00.

Solar State of the Union Report, a state-by-state listing of solar installations with comment on which states have good programs. Plus a list of cities and towns over 2,500 population indicating how many solar installations they should have to meet standards set by Congressional mandate under the Energy Act of 1978 (2.5 million solar homes by 1985). Only report of its kind in existence. $5.00.

Solar Energy Technical Training Directory. Solar Energy Research Institute, 1617 Cole Boulevard, Golden, Colorado 80401, (303) 231-1201. Lists 150 colleges and universities which offer training in solar system design, installation, and maintenance.

Solar Factsheet—Careers in the Solar Professions and Trades. National Solar Heating and Cooling Information Center, P.O. Box 1607, Rockville, Maryland 20850. Single copies free.

Starting Your Own Energy Business, 1978, Institute for Local Self Reliance, 1718 8th Street, N.W., Washington, D.C. 20009. $4.00. Provides information on starting small retail or manufacturing business in four fields: Retro-fitting, storm windows and doors, cellulose insulation, and solar hot water systems.

Note: Many states have departments of energy to which you can write to find out the state of the industry in your area.

Chapter 8

INFORMATION INDUSTRY CAREERS

What is the information industry? No industry by that name appears in the U.S. Department of Labor's *Occupational Outlook Handbook*. Yet, futurists like Peter Schwartz increasingly refer to it. Alfin Tofler in his book, *The Third Wave*,[1] said the first wave of civilization was based on agriculture, the second was based on manufacturing, and the third wave, which we are now entering, is based on information.

"The United States is rapidly shifting from a mass industrial society to an information society," says John Naisbitt, senior vice president of Yankelovich, Skelly and White, a firm of consultants on the future, and he has the figures to prove it. As late as 1950, 65 percent of our workers were in the industrial sector. That figure is already down to only 30 percent. In 1950 there were only 17 percent of workers in the information sector. Today it is better than 55 percent. "In the economy of the 1980s, more than half of our gross national product is based on development, storage, transfer and use of information," says Congressman Timothy E. Wirth, Chairman of the House Telecommunications Subcommittee.

Information is becoming the central feature of an entirely new age, sometimes referred to as the post-industrial era. In this new "information economy" the central activity which advances human welfare is processing information, just as manufacturing was the central activity of the industrial age.

One reason the information industry is not discussed in the *Occupational Outlook Handbook* is the fact that it has not yet coalesced as an industry. Nevertheless, information/knowledge occupations which were about 177 in 1950 are now up to about 607 and climbing. The vast communications field is only a part of the total infor-

---

[1] Tofler, Alfin, *The Third Wave*, William Morrow and Co., Inc., New York, 1980.

mation industry. (The newest developments in Communications will be discussed in a later volume in this series.) Like communications, however, information and its handling and use is so pervasive of every aspect of our lives, that it is difficult to identify as a separate industry.

Volumes could be written on the information industry. Here we shall discuss only a few of the new aspects of the information economy which are already becoming a part of every American's lifestyle. We will also look at the basic concepts helping to turn us from an industrial to an information society.

Computers—Chief Tool and Power Source

Peter Drucker, in his book, *The Age of Discontinuity*, says, "There is a great deal more to information and data processing than the computer. The computer is to the information industry roughly what the central power station is to the electric industry."[1] However, computers are both the major tool and the prime power source.

Computers make possible the handling of complex information systems and are a recent development of the industrial machine age. They were at first widely distrusted, seen as depersonalizing forces reducing people to electric impulses recorded and stored on tapes or disks. However, they developed so rapidly that they have become the means by which people receive more and more individualized services. For example, computerized banking can offer customers interest on checking accounts where both principal and rate may change daily. More and more banks use electronic tellers—computerized systems which provide banking services for the customer with access to the accounts 24 hours a day. What each customer wants and needs can be individually programmed with far more precision than ever before.

When you wish to check on an airline reservation, a few buttons pressed into a machine flashes on a screen your full itinerary and related details.

Data processing now permits businesses to handle their purchase orders, billing, inventories, tax, and employee benefit records, etc., with less personnel and more speed. Chapter 2 cited some of the expanding job opportunities in this area.

Understanding the computer as a power source compared to an electric power station is a little more difficult. Yet like electricity in

---

[1] Drucker, Peter F., *The Age of Discontinuity*, New York, 1978, p. 24.

the early 20th century, the use of computers has spread in every aspect of life.

A final block to unlimited expansion according to Peter Drucker is the development of a more comprehensive computer language. "We have to have a 'notation' comparable to the one St. Ambrose invented 1,600 years ago to record music, that expresses words and thoughts in symbols appropriate to the electric pulses rather than in the clumsy computer language of today."[1] Congitive scientists working with computer experts are rapidly getting around the problem by developing computers that have oral language capacity.

The Information Explosion

By the year 2000 there will be four times as much available information as in 1980. Two-thirds of the total content of that body of knowledge will be new, different or updated facts from what we have today. All of the knowledge available in 1979, according to a brochure sent out by the University and College Placement Association, represents only about 3 percent of what will be available in 50 years.

"For knowledge, too, is itself a power," said Sir Francis Bacon in the early 17th century. Today's futurists would agree. Control of land and available manpower was the basis for power in the agricultural ages. Control of raw materials and available manpower was the basis for power in the industrial era. Control of knowledge and the means to distribute knowledge is becoming the central economic resources of our time.

Information Science—Making Information Serve Society

The very fact that the American Society for Information Science has existed since 1937 shows that we are already well into this new information era. A recent brochure on *Super Careers in Information Science* said,

> "Information is any knowledge gained through communication, research, instruction, observation, etc. 'Information Science' is the study of the characteristics of information and how it is transferred or handled. It is concerned with the way people create, collect, organize, label, store, find, analyze, send, receive, and use information in making decisions. Information

---

[1] *Ibid.*, p. 25.

Science emphasizes the application of modern technologies—the interconnection of procedures, machines, and people—to assist in the transfer and handling information."

This association has some 4,000 members with some 23 different special interest areas including automated language processing, biological and chemical information systems, energy and environment information, information generation and publishing, library automation and networks, management of information activities, medical information systems, and non-print media.

Members of the Society are concerned with four general areas: The operation of information systems, the management of information systems, design of information systems, or research and teaching. The specific kinds of jobs to be found in each of these areas are of interest to all who want to be in the ground swell of the new information age. We include them as they appear in the A.S.I.S. bulletin quoted above.

1. Operation of Information Systems

Abstractor-Indexer	Processing the intellectual content of documents for convenient retrieval.
Bibliographic Searcher	Using modern computerized information systems and data bases, in batch or online mode, to identify or retrieve pertinent publications.
Database Manager	Analyzing, manipulating, and coordinating "hard" data for efficient use by researchers and management.
Information Broker	Performing specialized information retrieval services on a fee basis.
Information Marketing Specialist	Disseminating information on products and services available in the information industry.
Librarian	Collecting, organizing, and providing information.
Media Specialist	Using non-print technologies (audiovisual aids, television, microforms, films, tapes, etc.) to expedite the flow of information.

Records Manager	Maintaining systematic control of paperwork and records activities from their creation to final disposition.
Technical Information Manager	Using one's subject background to assist colleagues in satisfying their information requirements.
Technical Writer or Editor	Conveying technical information clearly to other technical audiences or the lay person.

2. Management of Information Systems

Information Center Manager	Supervising facilities that organize knowledge of a specific subject area.
Information Manager	Managing information systems and providing information services, information storage and retrieval, records management, and consulting on information problems within the organization.

3. Design of Information Systems

Application or Systems Programmer	Writing large-scale computer programs or modifying existing programs to solve information problems in business, science, education, etc.
Information Consultant	Advising management on development, marketing strategy, and business expansion through technology information systems.
Information Systems Engineer	Design, implementing, and evaluating new ways of organizing and distributing information.
Management Information Systems Specialist	Designing and implementing automated systems to satisfy the information needs of decision-makers.
Theasaurus-Designer	Developing a controlled list of terms and conceptually associated terms for use in information-retrieval systems.

4. Research and Teaching

Computational Linguist	Analyzing word and language structure to determine how the computer can manipulate text for indexing, classification, abstracting, search and retrieval.
Cyberneticist	Studying communication and manipulation of information and its use in controlling the behavior of biological, physical and chemical systems.
Information Scientist	Conducting basic research on the phenomena of information.
Education and Training Specialist	Providing an interface between a user and a system, communications network or database.
Teacher of Information Studies	Educating others in the planning, designing, management, evaluation, and use of the total information process.

The Information Industry Association (316 Pennsylvania Avenue, S.E., Suite 502, Washington, D.C. 20003) founded in 1969, has over 800 members. It recently set up a special program called AIM, *Associated Information Managers*, to which many information professionals working in business and industry belong.

Consulting or the Selling of Information

It is not surprising that as the age of information develops there has been a parallel explosive growth of consultants of all kinds. One of the earliest types were public relations consultants. Early practitioners were usually transplants from the newspaper industry—by the late 1930s they began transferring their developed skills in writing, plus their knowledge of the public interests to what was then an entirely new field. The Public Relations Society of America, founded in 1948, works to develop standards for the field and increase its professionalism. In the early 1980s, there were an estimated 120,000 public relations workers. They handle many of the information and communications problems for businesses and corporations, trade and professional associations, labor unions, schools and colleges, government agencies, non-profit agencies, and individuals.

More than 300 college and universities offer at least one course in public relations today. Some 50 institutions offer special programs in public relations.

Public relation jobs are varied and carry many titles. They include public information, investor relations, public affairs, corporate communications, employee relations, marketing and product publicity, consumer service or customer relations. Basic to all of these is handling information and planning communications of information in all different media.

What the public relations worker sells, whether working directly for an organization or operating as a consultant, is a combination of skills such as writing, and a knowledge of one or more media areas. A few PR experts have become so successful that they sell only their expert opinions on specific communication problems of clients. They leave the carrying out of the public relations program to others.

Consultants

Consulting is one of the world's oldest professions. When you consult your doctor or lawyer, you are buying what is in their heads. You seek their expert opinion based on relevant education and experience, plus usually, their skill. A few highly experienced professionals have moved away from selling their hands-on-skill toward pure consulting—selling their knowledge and judgment only. Knowledge and skills are so closely related in solving any problem that it will probably never be possible to separate them completely. However, as we move further into the information age, more and more stress will be laid on higher degrees of specialized education. Research and development professors in universities have often spent their whole lives in study and experimentation. Yet they are frequently called upon for the knowledge they can contribute—especially in rapidly developing fields such as electronics, computer science, and information science. In general, one does not become a consultant of any kind without first becoming an excellent practitioner in the particular area.

Along with the information explosion has come an explosion in the different kinds of consultants who make a living by selling information. Unusual examples include the following:

— Personal image consultant: advises people on how to dress, how to speak and act in public, and how to get attention using personal publicity. This young industry already has a *Directory of*

Personal Image Consultants (published by the Editorial Service Company, 1140 Avenue of the Americas, New York, N.Y. 10036. $3.95).

— Leisure Consultant: guides people who can't decide what to do with their free time. More than 380 colleges offer majors in leisure studies. The National Parks and Recreation Association says that leisure consulting is provided by at least 150 institutions ranging from veterans hospitals to juvenile-detention centers. *The Wall Street Journal* interviewed a number of leisure counselors and reported excellent business and active practices.

— Management Consultant: recommends the best and most up-to-date operating procedures to client businesses and organizations. The growing complexity of business stimulates need for management consultants. They help companies solve problems arising from government regulations, rapid technological change, development of foreign markets, etc. Two associations, Association of Consulting Management Engineers and the Institute of Management Consultants, work to upgrade and further professionalize consultants. The Institute offers the CMC, Certified Management Consultant status, to qualified members. Standards are constantly being strengthened and a testing program for certification is under study.

— Retirement Consultant: Retirement counseling programs are spreading fast as companies grapple with a rapidly growing problem: fear of retiring. The American Association of Retired Persons reports that over 900 companies use an eight-session program developed by AARP.

— Investment Consultant: Financial counselors are found in investment firms or in private practice. Once used only by the very rich, the investment counselor's services are now widely used by middle-class Americans seeking to preserve the little wealth they have achieved, against the incroachments of inflation. A financial counselor in Hawaii was recently reported to charge $1,200 a hour for his services.

— Job Hunting Coach: A form of counseling for college graduates who can't find jobs, job coaches, charge from $35 to $3,000 to tell graduates how to conduct themselves in a job interview, including such details as what to wear, and how to drive a salary offer up. They also suggest potential employers or sources of job leads.

— Puppetry Consultant: The consultants at the Puppetry Resource Institute in San Francisco earn from $50 to $100 a day for combining puppetry with education. They advise people wishing to enter the field, where to find training, and gain needed experience.

— Professional Grandmother Consultant: A group of pediatricians in La Jolla, California, has added a grandmother to its staff to provide child care advice to parents who do not have the advantages of an extended family.

— Costume Consultant: During our country's recent Bicentennial celebration a costume consultant provided advice on the proper 18th century design for both men's and women's clothing, drafted many patterns, and constructed a few of the garments.

— Party Consultant: A number of people have gone into the party planning business. They advise both corporate and private party givers on everything—the theme, the invitations, what to serve, how to decorate, where to locate catering services, etc. Once the basic decisions are made concerning the party, the consultant handles all the problems of obtaining needed services and supplies and arranges the schedule.

Advocates

Another group of persons whose chief activity is to provide specialized information to those in need are the advocates. In recent years a number of different types have emerged—consumer advocates, human rights advocates, child advocates and welfare rights advocates to name a few.

Advocates are used in the same way as consultants. They are expected to assist with the solution of the clients' problems. They place more emphasis on the need of their clients than on selling of information, *per se*. In general, they are strongly motivated to improve the lives of their clients. They often work for little or no pay to obtain for their clients, rights granted by existing laws, or to change policies or regulations which work against their clients' interests.

Advocates may have legal or social work backgrounds and educations. They often have emerged from positions in government or private agencies which put them in close contact with the kinds of people with problems they have the expertise to help solve.

Consumer advocates and human rights advocates frequently have legal backgrounds. They have seen first hand the ways the free market system or the justice system has been unfair to some of us. They have decided to devote their lives to improving the situation. They have a special interest in helping those who cannot pay the high cost of legal advice. Many public law firms are organized as non-profit organizations. This makes it possible for them to charge lower fees for helping clients with class action or other suits brought about through violation of consumer or rights regulations and laws.

Welfare rights advocates and child advocates frequently come from social work backgrounds. Their work has put them in close contact with the disadvantaged who often don't know how to obtain the benefits to which they are entitled. They also have seen many abused children who are under the legal jurisdiction of their parents, as are all minors, but who obviously are not cared for by them. Such children need child advocates.

Many government and private social service agencies now make sure that they have persons on their staffs who are capable of serving as advocates as the need arises. Often these are social workers. Occasionally, there is a staff lawyer who usually represents the agency rather than any of its clients. The social worker can turn the results of investigations over to a lawyer in a public law firm when the need arises for legal action.

Like individual consultants and advocates, consulting firms have been around for a long time. However, we are now beginning to see the rise of new businesses entirely devoted to providing information, usually not limited by any one subject area. One such firm, founded in Berkeley, California, calls itself "Information on Demand." According to its objective, "Information on Demand provides a full range of information gathering and organizing services to a broad spectrum of clients—from Fortune 500 companies to private individuals."

Training for Information Industry

Much of the training needed to become a full participant in some part of the vast new information industry is already available. However, in college catalogs, one does not usually find a department of information studies. The American Society for Information Science suggests that those attending colleges or universities which do not yet offer programs in information science might take a major in the behavioral sciences, and a minor in the computer science or vice versa. Courses selected from a number of core areas of study will prepare a student for a career in information science. These core areas include computer science; library science; behavioral science including psycology and sociology; engineering; communications including journalism, technical writing, printing, radio and television; and business administration. Requirements for entrance to graduate programs in information science vary, but most require a basic knowledge of mathematics and statistics, and computers and programming. The Society has prepared a list of 35 colleges and universities which offer graduate programs in information science. It is by no means exclusive but does include examples of the types of schools. In around 15 schools such programs are to be found in divisions of library science, library and information science, or just information science. The names vary somewhat. Several are schools or departments of computer science, or computer and information science. Today's librarians who wish to move ahead are becoming computer specialists. In other schools, the information science program may be linked with communications, engineering, medicine or business management.

Several things about occupations of the future become clear as we stand on the brink of the information age. Higher and higher degrees of education coupled with experience in one or more related fields will be necessary for those who reach the top. As we have seen above, higher education for the information sciences scarcely begins until graduate school. Advocates usually have worked as lawyers or social workers before becoming advocates. Consultants have first been successful communicators in newspapers or other media before becoming public relations professionals. A career as successful engineers, physicians, financial managers, administrators, or whatever is essential before turning to advising in those areas.

Computers are the most sophisticated machines to be developed in the waning industrial age. They are also the principle tool of the information age. Judging from the training that is emerging for information science, a blend of computer science and social science, it seems likely that computers will be the means of moving machines and people closer so that they can work in harmony to create a better lifestyle for us all. This becomes even more apparent when we realize that with available technology, the books, held by the Library of Congress in its many buildings, can be stored on discs in a room the size of a small auditorium.

Jobs With A Future

Abstractor-indexer
Advocate
Application or systems programmer
Archival administrator
Bibliographic searcher
Computational linguist
Consultant
Cyberneticist
Data base designer
Data base manager
Education and training specialist
Free lance librarian
Image consultant (speech, dress, public relations, motivation)
Information broker

Information center manager

Information consultant

Information coordinator

Information manager

Information marketing specialist

Information specialist

Information research scientist

Information scientist

Information systems engineer

Librarian

Library/information consultant

Management information systems
  specialist

Media specialist

Ombudsman or ombudswoman

Public relations specialist

Records manager

Teacher, information studies

Technical information manager

Technical information specialist

Technical writer or editor

Thesaurus designer

Word processing operator

For Further Information—Some starting points

American Business Communications Association, 911 S Sixth Street, Champaign, Illinois 61820. An organization concerned with instruction in communications.

American Communications Association, 111 Broadway, New York, N.Y. 10006, (212) 267-1374. A labor organization for communications personnel.

American Federation of Word Processing Societies, 1815 N Lynn Street, Suite 800, Arlington, Virginia 22209, (703) 558-3600. The Federation publishes "A Look Into Computer Careers," available free. Send a large stamped return addressed envelope.

American Society for Information Science, 1010 16th Street, N.W., Washington, D.C. 20036, (202) 659-3644. Provides information on graduate schools in this field.

American Word Processing Association, P.O. Box 16267, Lansing, Michigan 48901.

Associated Information Managers, 316 Pennsylvania Avenue, S.E., Suite 502, Washington, D.C. 20003, (202) 544-2893.

Association for Educational Communications and Technology, 1126 16th Street, N.W., Washington, D.C. 20036, (202) 833-4180.

Association for Systems Management, 24587 Bagley Road, Cleveland, Ohio 44136, (216) 243-6900.

Association of Information Dissemination Centers, P.O. Box 8105, Athens, Georgia 30603, (404) 542-3106.

Computer and Communications Industry Association, 1500 Wilson Boulevard, Suite 512, Arlington, Virginia 22209, (703) 534-1360.

Connell, Stephen and Ian A. Galbraith: *Electronic Mail: A Revolution in Business Communications.* White Plains, N.Y.: Knowledge Industry, 1982, 141 pp.

Council of Communications Societies, P.O. Box 1074, Silver Spring, Maryland 20910, (301) 953-7100. Publishes *Communications Notes* newsletter.

Data Processing Management Association, 505 Busse Highway, Park Ridge, Illinois 60068. Publishes "Your Career in Data Processing," available free. Send a large stamped, return addressed envelope.

Davis, Charles and James E. Rush: *Guide to Information Science*. Westport, Connecticut: Greenwood, 1980, 305 pp.

Debos, Anthony King, Donald W. King, Una Mansfield, and Donald L. Shirey: *The Information Professional—Survey of an Emerging Field*. Marcel Dekker, Inc., 1981.

Encyclopedia of Information Systems and Services. Detroit: Gale Research Company, 1981, 1,000 pp.

Evan, William M. (editor): *Knowledge and Power in a Global Society*. Beverly Hills: Sage Publications, 1981.

Fusdick, Howard, *Computer Basics for Librarians and Information Scientists*. Arlington, Virginia: Information Resources Press, 1981.

Garvith, Andrew P. and Herbert Bermuni: *How to Win with Information or Lose Without It*. Bermuni Books, 815 15th Street, N.W., Washington, D.C. 20003, 1980.

Health Science Communications Association, P.O. Box 1207, Milledgeville, Georgia 31061. Operates a clearinghouse for information about the health field.

Hounsel, Dai et al.: *Educational Information and the Teacher*. New York: State Mutual Books and Distribution Service, 1980.

Industrial Communication Council, P.O. Box 3970, Grand Central Station, New York, N.Y. 10163, (212) 661-5080.

Information Industry Association, 316 Pennsylvania Avenue, S.E., Suite 400, Washington, D.C. 20003, (301) 654-4150. The *IIA Membership Directory* lists over 125 companies in this field.

Information Industry Market Place. R. R. Bowker Company, 1180 Avenue of the Americas, New York, New York 10036, (212) 764-5100. This $35.00 book is found in major libraries and lists 2,500 firms and other organizations in the information field.

International Communication Association, 10100 Burnet Road, Austin, Texas 78758, (512) 836-0440.

International Information/Word Processing Association, 1015 N. York Road, Willow Grove, Pennsylvania 19090, (215) 651-3220.

Joint Council on Educational Telecommunications, 1126 16th Street, N.W., Washington, D.C. 20036, (202) 659-9740. This is an organization of broadcasting groups.

Lamberton, D.M. (Edited by Meherod Jussawallin): *Communications Economics and Development*. Elmsford, New York: Pergaman Press, 1982.

Library and Information Technology Association (a division of the American Library Association), 50 E. Huron Street, Chicago, Illinois 60611.

McDaniel, Herman: *Careers in Computer and Data Processing*. New York: Petrocelli Books, 1978, 175 pp.

Maramhian, Oirig and Richard W. Boss: *Fee Based Information Services: A Study of a Growing Industry.* New York: R. R. Bowker Company, 1980.

Masuda, Youmeji: *The Information Society as Post Industrial Society.* Institute for the Information Society, Jujimura Building, 2-15-25 Tokyo, Japan, 341-8515, 1981.

National Black Media Coalition, 2027 Massachusetts Avenue, N.W., Washington, D.C. 20036, (202) 797-7473.

Public Relations Society of America, 845 Third Avenue, New York, N.Y., 10010, (212) 826-1750.

Schoech, Dick: *Computer Use in Human Services: A Guide to Information Management.* New York: Human Sciences Press, 1982.

Society for Information Display, 654 Sepelveda Boulevard, Los Angeles, California 90049, (213) 472-3550.

Spivak, James F. *Careers in Information.* White Plains, N.Y.: Knowledge Industry Publications, 1982.

Super Careers in Information Science, American Society for Information Science, 1010 16th Street, N.W., Washington, D.C. 20036, 1981.

Synott, William R. and William H. Gruber: *Information Resource Management: Opportunities and Strategies for the 1980's.* New York: Wiley-Interspace, 1981.

Tuu, Julius T. (edited by): *Advances in Information Systems Science,* New York: Plenum Press, 1979.

Who's Who in Information Management, AIM Membership Directory, 1981-82, 316 Pennsylvania Avenue, S.E., Suite 400, Washington, D.C., (202) 544-1969.

Women in Communications, P.O. Box 9561, Austin, Texas 78766. There are 150 chapters all over the country.

Word Processing Management Association, P.O. Box 87452, Chicago, Illinois 90980.

Word Processing Society, P.O. Box 92553, Milwaukee, Wisconsin 53202, (414) 276-8835.

Note: There are several hundred associations listed under "data processing." To find your special interest group consult an associations directory at your public library.

Chapter 9

OCEAN INDUSTRY CAREERS: OCEAN MINING, OFF-SHORE OIL PRODUCTION, EXPLORATION, AND RESEARCH

Fishing the seas for food or traveling over them to trade are occupations almost as old as the human race. How can the ocean industries rate a place among "the newest of the new?" The answer is very clear. Marine technology is making possible many things in and on the oceans that were never possible before. Ocean mining, fish-farming, mineral reclamation, oil prospecting, treasure hunting, and underwater archeology are just a few which have made the headlines lately. The interests of many old and long established professions, as well as some quite new ones are quite literally running into the oceans these days.

The Marine Technology Society recently sponsored a meeting and called the 1980s "The Decade of the Oceans." A list of participating societies gives a glimpse of the breath of interest in this new area including the American Association for the Advancement of Science, American Chemical Society (Geochemistry Division), American Geophysical Union, American Institute of Aeronautics and Astronautics, Inc., American Institute of Chemical Engineers, Society of Naval Architects and Marine Engineers, National Association of Corrosion Engineers, Sea Grant Association, Shipbuilders Council of America, Acoustical Society of America, and the National Estuarine Foundation. Some government agencies are also very much into the ocean sciences—including the Fish and Wildlife Services and the National Marine Fisheries Service of the Department of the Interior, the U.S. Army Corps of Engineers, the National Oceanic and Atmospheric Administration of the Department of Commerce and the Woods Hole Oceanographic Institution (a private organization which works mainly on U.S. government contracts).

More than 40 companies—mostly manufacturers of specialty

equipment, plus a few government agencies and universties exhibited at the Marine Technology Conference. Their sessions focused on such topics as oceanographic ships, buoy technology, unmanned vehicles, diving, remote sensing, off-shore structures, oil pollution, radioactive waste, water quality, ocean mining, undersea physics, and sea floor engineering. All of these fields offer fascinating new and emerging careers.

Admiral John B. Hayes, Commandant of the U.S. Coast Guard, who chaired the meeting, summed it all up:

> "This year's theme, 'The Decade of the Oceans,' has been selected because it represents both a turning point and an opportunity for a new perspective in the many dimensions of marine technology. In the coming years, the United States, as well as other nations, must turn to the oceans and coastal areas to develop living and non-living resources to meet our critical requirements. Significant socio-environmental concerns must be carefully considered during the planning and resource development process."

Obviously there are many new careers already existing in the industries which are developing the tools for the "Decade of the Oceans." Now let's take a closer look at some of these emerging career areas.

Ocean Mining

Ocean mining can be defined as the bringing to the surface and processing of millions of tons of mineral-rich nodules which lie on the ocean floors in deposits of varying thickness. Ocean mining is not yet in commercial operation, but research and development indicates that it is clearly possible.

The existence of mineral-rich sea nodules was discovered by the British in the early 1870s. A research sailing ship was sent on a 79,000 mile journey to study the world's oceans and routine dredging brought up what they called "concretionary lumps." They were reddish-brown to black lumps ranging in size from cinders to charred potatoes and were made of metal oxides. At first they were regarded mainly as curiosities and put on view at the British Museum.

Sometime after World War II, when underwater cameras were improved, it became clear that millions of square miles of ocean floor are literally paved with these black nodules. The majority rest in the soft sedimentary ooze 10,000 to 20,000 feet beneath the ocean surface. Mineral content varies somewhat, but the majority are rich in manganese (up to 30%) with some copper, nickel, and cobalt. They are richer than many ores mined conventionally on land. Business leaders in the industrialized countries were quick to see this vast potential. Several international consortia of oil, mining, and metal manufacturing companies were formed in the 1970s to develop ocean mining.

Oceanographic surveys show that one of the heaviest concentrations of nodules lies in a strip approximately 2,500 miles long and 500 miles wide, stretching from west of Mexico to south of Hawaii. Major consortia are prospecting in this area for suitable claim sites, but three difficult problems remain to be solved. How can the nodules be retrieved? What will their collection and processing do to the environment? Many new and successful careers await those scientists and engineers who contributes to any of these solutions. And who, if anyone, owns these minerals?

The technology of ocean mining is developing. The consortia are experimenting with three different approaches: the vacuum cleaner, the bucket brigade, and the water beetle. The vacuum cleaner sucks up the nodules similar to the way sand is sucked up to remove the overload around sunken ships. The bucket brigade uses a long chain of buckets dragged along the bottom and continuously rotated to the surface. The water beetle is a remote controlled unmanned vehicle which could be sent down equipped with special scoops. Unmanned vehicles have already been developed to accomplish numerous tasks on the moon and their adaptation for underwater use is under way. Solutions to any remaining technological problems will probably emerge in a straight-forward, uncomplicated sequence until the most efficient answers are found.

Answers to the problem of ecology and ownership rights are far more complex. This vast new source of mineral wealth which has now become technologically retrievable, lies in international waters. By long accepted international law, these waters are open to all. Although the oceans concern almost every country in the world, we have only one international organization in a position to develop agreements. The United Nations began working in the mid-1970s on a "Law of the Seas" treaty. This is a global political effort to create some controls for roughly three-quarters of the Earth's surface which is covered by oceans. The new treaty operates on the assumption that the nodules are not the property of the first countries with the technology to take them, but rather the heritage of all mankind to be regulated solely by a proposed U.N. seabed authority. This authority would license private companies to mine but only in tandem with a U.N. ocean-mining company. Royalties would go to underdeveloped countries. Strict limits would regulate the production of ocean metals so that land-based mines (many in underdeveloped countries) would not suffer price competition with this new industry with its plentiful resources.

The ocean-mining consortia fear that all these rules, regulations, and assessments might make it economically impossible to mine the oceans. The most unacceptable provision to free market countries is that participating companies must share openly (give away) all their technology and trade secrets, not only to the U.N. company but to any U.N. member nation desiring to go into the ocean mining field. The United States did not sign the U.N. Law of the Sea treaty. Rather, in 1982, U.S. and three Western countries signed an agreement on deep-sea mining claims. France, Great Britain, West Germany and the United States agreed to resolve through consultations any conflicting claims made by sea-bed mining consortia members under the existing laws of each country. The agreements does not preclude the other countries from signing the U.N. treaty.

That is the situation at the present time. Ocean mining stands in a sort of political limbo. Many companies from Western countries have done research and development and prospecting and stand ready to start mining almost any time. A few analysts have suggested that if no acceptable international treaty is signed, a kind of sea mining piracy will develop. Others question whether nodules will ever be mined.

The excitement about ocean mining, however, refuses to go away. Bill Siapno, head of marine sciences for Deepsea Ventures, a consortium backed firm whose goal is to retrieve three million tons a year of manganese nodules, compares it to the pioneering spirit of those who left St. Louis in covered wagons. "Everything about it is all trial and all new," he says, "and deep ocean mining—the last great gold rush—is even newer." Given the world's increasing need for, and decreasing supply of minerals, his enthusiasm is probably well founded.

Off-Shore Oil Prospecting and Production

Off-shore drilling in waters surrounding the United States proceeded directly and quite literally from on-shore drilling. In 1886, H. L. Williams drilled for oil on the beach Southwest of Santa Barbara. Williams was successful and became an oil millionaire. But indications were that access to the oil would be even better over the water. The first drilling for oil over water was done from wharves as early as 1902. By 1930, they were drilling from piers and from off-shore structures set on pilings like overseas causeways. Then a mobile platform was developed, a barge which could be moved, with the capability of drilling deeper than 100 fathoms. Since 1947, off-shore drilling platforms resting on the sea floor have dominated this area.

According to the American Petroleum Institute, there are four different methods for off-shore drilling used today. Which one is used depends upon the particular set of circumstances.

1. A floating vessel moored above the well site.
2. A semi-submersible vessel floating above the sea bottom.
3. A "jack-up," where steel rigs are placed on the bottom and the drilling platform is jacked up above the waves.
4. A steel or concrete platform extending from the seabed to a height safely above the storm waves.

Permanent platforms of the latter type are designed to withstand storms of the greatest intensity ever recorded over the previous 100 years in the specific areas where they are located. A number of separate wells may be drilled from a single platform. Drilling platforms at sea generally have fully equipped living quarters for the crews. They also have heliports which connect the residents with their mainland bases.

Between now and the late 1980s we shall be drilling in deeper and deeper water as we exhaust reserves under the continental shelf. Development of new platforms to meet new circumstances goes on constantly. One has been developed by Exxon. This is a new type of tower to support a drilling platform which can be used in waters over 1,000 feet deep. It is called a guyed tower and will be less expensive to construct in deep water than steel and concrete platforms. The theory behind the guyed tower is that such a structure does not have to be as massive and rigid as a steel and concrete platform if it can be made to comply with wind, waves, and currents. The guyed tower has a relatively light metal skeleton which sits upright on the bottom, and on which the platform is built. It stands upright in the water guyed by six heavy cables which are bolted to the sea floor in a wide circle around the tower.

Two things keep it upright and resistant to storm waves. One is a new system of "clump weights" placed near the bottom ends of the cables. By picking up the slack in the guy cables, they help offset the rise and fall of the ocean waves. The other is a system of air-filled buoyancy tanks 100 feet long which are attached to the tower under water near the top.

One such guyed platform now nearing completion has a three-level, 75,000 square foot deck. It will accommodate production drilling, a maximum of 54 wells can be drilled from the tower and producing operations. The platform will have living quarters for more than 40 people.

A second very different type of new drilling platform has been developed for use on the North Slopes of Alaska. In addition to the usual engineering, geological, and oceanological problems, there is the primary problem of protecting the workmen who have to operate outdoors in temperatures which may reach −40° F for weeks on end.

This new rig, known as Rig 29-E, was built for Sohio Alaska Company. Like most Arctic drilling facilities, it has a mast covered with thick windwalls around the lower section to protect the workers. Adjacent to the derrick is a complex of prefabricated buildings that house the tools and workers. The big difference is that this whole assembly is mounted on wheels taller than a man. The drilling unit consists of five sections mounted on wheeled trailer frames. Each trailer has its own self-jacking hydraulic system so that the entire section can be simply picked up and hooked onto a large truck or tractor for quick haul from well to well on land or over ice in winter.

Roughnecks working on this new rig have to spend much less time outside. Not only has it improved their working conditions but their productivity as well, in what has to be one of the world's most rigorous jobs. Roughnecks on the North Slope can earn up to $70,000 a year.

Improvements are constantly being made in each of the four basic methods of drilling. This makes it possible to drill further and further from shore, to drill much deeper, and to recover a larger percentage of the oil found. The roughnecks who work on these platforms are often transplanted from land operations. But off shore drilling employs a vast variety of other scientists, specialists and technicians used also in other parts of the ocean industries.

Deep Sea Exploration and Research

The term, plate tectonics, has only been used in scientific circles for a few years. It represents an exciting new concept of the origins of the Earth. What makes it particularly exciting is that it is a theory that can be and is being proven daily. Plate tectonics views the Earth's crust, on which both landmasses and the oceans rest, as consisting of six to eight reasonably well defined plates. These are cracked pieces of the Earth's crust if you will. They adjoin each other. They are in constant motion, thrusting, grinding, and overriding one another like ice flows in an arctic sea. Bits and pieces of evidence which support the concept have been emerging through research in many different fields for more than twenty years.

People have speculated on how the world began since the beginning of time. In the Middle Ages and well into the 19th century "deluvianists" reasoned that all fossils were caused by the Great Flood recorded in the Old Testament, which was believed to have happened in the year 2349 B.C. In 1650 an archbishop, the primate of all Ireland, established that the world and everything in it begun at 9:00 a.m. on Sunday, the twenty-third of October in the year 4004 B.C.

Benjamin Franklin guessed from what he saw that the interior of the Earth might consist of "a fluid more dense . . . than any of the solids we are acquainted with. Thus the surface of the globe would be a shell capable of being broken and disordered by the violent movements in the fluids on which it rested."

Up until recently there was no way that any of these theories could be tested. Some things had been learned by land based geologists and paleontologists. Since land covers only one third of the Earth, and water the other two thirds, this gave us a sketchy picture at best.

The concept that continents move (called "continental drift") got some publicity in the 1920s and 1930s. It was, by then, held to be possible but not provable.

By the 1950s scientific instrumentation and technologies had developed sufficiently to begin to prove or disprove theories about continental movement. But this was only a secondary purpose of the development. In the early 1950s, spurred by World War II and the tensions of the Cold War, the British developed an improved magnetometer for protection against submarines. Later it proved even more useful in deep sea research. New deep ocean sounding devices were developed. Great strides were made in improving underwater photography and in sea floor core drilling machinery and sampling techniques. The United States Navy undertook a gigantic project to map the world's ocean floors. Ships of many of our allies cooperated. Information began to pour in from thousands of ships and oceanographic vessels on soundings being made all over the world. One of the early discoveries was that there is a continuous 47,000 mile long undersea chain of smooth and jagged ridges that meander about the entire globe. These are literally mountain ranges under the sea higher than any we have on land. Variations in the ocean's depth were known before this, of course. But they were vaguely conceived of as gentle rises in the ocean's floor.

Now previous assumptions, prevalent in geology texts of the day, were being challenged with first-hand research. One accepted theory was that there could be no life in the deepest parts of the ocean because of the tremendous water pressures at that depth. Underwater cameras and bathosphere explorations, however, revealed that there is indeed a whole variety of colorful marine life in the ocean at every depth.

Core samples of the ocean floors taken at ever deepening levels disproved the commonly accepted belief that there would be a tremendously deep formation of sediment and under that layers of rock in the same geological order as found on land. But core samples from the deepest levels revealed relatively new volcanic rock and surprisingly little sediment. Underwater photographs taken of lava flows showed patterns similar to those caused when hot lava is plunged into very cold water.

Once it became possible to scientifically study the earth under the seas, many land-based geologists were able to contribute knowledge. Seismologists were able to locate the world's thousands of volcanos on both land and sea. They pointed out that volcanos as well as most earthquakes occurred along lines which were then being located and defined as the edges of techtonic plates—places where different parts of the earth's surface come together and grind against each other.

Some progress is being made on the question of what moves the plates? The best thinking of geologists, physicists, and engineers seems to be that it is some form of convection current operating in the more viscous layers of the Earth. It is understood that such a convection current would have to operate in substances more dense than those with which we have had experience. However, much of what the seismologists are learning would support the convection theory.

Seismologists read records of Earth vibrations on their seismographs. They have learned to use earthquake vibrations like X-rays to construct a cross-sectional picture of the Earth's interior. This is possible because earthquake waves travel at different speeds through material of differing densities. Earthquake waves also reflect when they encounter boundaries between layers of differing consistences. Seismologists note these reflections and measure the differences in time it takes the earthquake vibrations to travel around the Earth's crust compared with the time it takes to travel directly through the Earth. They are able to deduce that the Earth's interior is made of concentric layers of varying consistences. The picture is something like this: The Earth's crust, on which we live, is only about 100 miles thick, relatively cool at 52 degrees near the surface. Next comes the mantle layer, some 1,000 miles thick. It is part vuscous, part molten and ranges in temperature from 2300 to 5900 degrees F. Finally, there is the 2,700 mile thick core with temperature ranges from around 7000 to 8600 degrees F.

So, the Earth, at its intermost, is a furnace to surpass all furnaces. It is thought to be fueled by the decay of radio active materials mainly uranium, thorium, and potassium. Ben Franklin was not so far off. The convection theory as a source of plate movement seems more plausable after all this research.

Water was the first fluid with which we observed the convection theory in action, warm water currents rising, cold water currents falling. Water has a density of 1. The lower mantle density ranges from 5.7 to 3.3. The upper mantle on which the plates may float, has a density of 1.1. Could the techtonic plates be moving on a convection current in the upper mantle? The scientific community now presumes that they do but much more research is needed.

All the action we observe on the Earth's surface really takes place at the point where the crust interfaces with the mantle. Volcanic eruptions were probably the first such action mankind observed. Science now permits us to view evidence of hot lava welling up in the deep trenches under the sea to cause sea-floor spreading. We hear about disasterous earthquakes on the South American West coast where the plate on which the South American continent rides is overriding the plate on which the Eastern Pacific Ocean rides. Pressure from the overridden plate not only accounts for earthquakes and volcano eruptions, but helps explain the process of mountain building which has long been noted by geologists. Material being overridden is probably re-melted into hot upper-mantle thus balancing out the total volume being created by sea floor spreading.

In the past ten years plate tectonics has provided an exploding amount of information which embraces much of the fields of geology, oceanography, and earth science. It has spawned a wide variety of super-specialists, for example, paleomagneticians. And it has laid the scientific foundations for rapid advances in the fields as widely apart as ocean mining, off-shore drilling, underwater archeology, and treasure hunting. All these fields have contributed to, and make use of technology and equipment developed for operating under water.

Research in the ocean sciences is an expanding field, and its technology is growing apace.

The Job Outlook:

Persons currently engaged in these exciting new areas of ocean mining, off-shore drilling, and deep sea exploration have various combinations of education and skills. Petroleum geology, marine technology, and engineering are all important to off-shore drilling personnel. Oceanography, marine technology, geology, seismology, marine engineering, and meteorology are just some of the fields of knowledge needed for development of ocean mining or underwater research. Top positions in underwater research, and also in the other two areas, are often occupied by highly educated specialists with training and skills in more than one area. Just as with others discussed in this book, the key to the top is usually multidisciplinary.

Note: Resources on the Ocean Industries appear at the end of Chapter 10.

Chapter 10

OCEAN INDUSTRY CAREERS: UNDERWATER ARCHEOLOGY, AQUACULTURE, AND SUBMERSIBLES

Underwater Archeology and Treasuring Hunting

There is a good reason for linking together the subjects in this section. The treasure that one finds in wrecks of ancient ships consists of artifacts of the period when the ship sailed. These can be sold for very high prices to museums, to the governments of the countries involved, or to private collectors. Treasure hunting can be profitable. Treasure hunters today use the most modern underwater techniques to discover, raise, and preserve the artifacts, and sometimes the ship itself intact.

Willard Bascomb, former chairman of the board of Ocean Sciences and Engineering, Inc., of Long Beach, California, explains why such treasures are so valuable.

> "Every ship is a small sample of the life and times during which it sailed. On ancient ships, as on today's ships, the people aboard had all the utensils required for living, the weapons for fighting, and the tools for working. . . . Since each ship represents the surrounding civilization, and since most sink quickly, carrying down everything except minor flotsam, a complete ancient ship in good condition is the marine archeologist's dream—a sort of under-sea Pompeii in which dark, cold water instead of hot ashes has preserved a moment in time."

Finding artifacts under the sea in relatively shallow water is not new. In 1832, the fifth century Bronze Apollo, which now stands in the Louvre, was brought up by a trawler from the waters off the island of Elba. This and other spectacular art finds under the Mediterranean excited the art world but were archeologically less important in defining societies and cultures. There was nothing very scientific about these early explorations. Relics found were regarded mainly as curiosities, they rarely could be related to the culture, technology, or civilization which they had survived.

It is a fact of nature that many interesting and valuable things can survive under the sea for as long as 2,000 years. According to Willard Bascomb, they include such things as metal ingots (bronze, tin, copper, gold and silver), tools, coins, amphorae (large pottery jugs in which olive oil and other liquids were shipped), pottery, glass and inscribed stone tablets. Ship's gear which may survive includes anchors, bronze tools, tiles, utensils, metal fasteners, ballast rocks, firepots, leg-irons, navigational equipment, and lead sheeting. Military equipment (if made of bronze) includes armor, swords, spears, shields, helmets, chariots, axes, boarding grapples, Greek fire tubes, and ramming beaks. Art objects often include sarcophagi, columns, statues of bronze, stone or clay, bracelets, rings and other jewelry and muscial instruments.

The best preserved and most complete sunken ships are those which have been buried in the mud or silt for hundreds or thousands of years. Until recently no technology was available to recover things from such deep water or, for that matter, even to locate them.

By the early 1950s, however, more oceanographic ships were being built and especially equipped for research. Among the earliest to apply marine technology to excavating wrecked ships was Jaques Y. Cousteau. In 1952 he organized a team of divers to excavate a wreck at Gran Conloue near Marsailles. The Cousteau group, then and later, pioneered many techniques that have since greatly refined underwater exploration including the use of television, air lifts, and the Aqualung. By the late 1950s a technology for precise excavation of wrecks in shallow water had been established.

The "treasure hunt" often starts at libraries or archives to search out old shipping routes, shipping schedules, and records of sunken vessels. Once the ship has been located on the ocean floor, there is still much to be done before any excavation takes place. Various types of surveys can now be made using sonar, transponders, and sounding devices. Underwater photographs are taken, and television is used. The floor over and for some distance around the wreck is marked off into squares called the reference grid. Each square is systematically excavated and the precise location where each item is found is marked on a survey grid map aboard the support ship.

What is being done today archeologically under the seas is extremely thorough and productive. And discoveries are being made in every corner of the globe. Here are just a few examples:

1. In 1961, the *Vassa*, a 17th century Swedish warship which sank in 1628, was raised from the muddy bottom of Stockholm harbor. It's complete hull was well preserved.

2. In 1962, the Roskilde Viking ships, sunk about 1400 A.D. were raised from a Danish harbor. At least one complete Viking ship has been raised, restored and placed in a museum. The process necessitated lengthy chemical treatment of the wood so that it would not disintegrate now that it is back in an air environment.

3. In the early 1970s, the wreck of the *Monitor* was located. This famous, iron-clad Civil War ship was sunk in 1862 off Cape Hatteras, North Carolina. There were full records of its final hours, but locating it in the traditional "graveyard of ships" was not easy. Once it was located and surveyed with still and television cameras, the decision was made that it was too far gone with rust and decay to be raised. However, some remarkable photographs of the wreck have added to our records of the Civil War.

4. In 1978, excavations were in progress of an ancient ship in a narrow passage between Turkey and the Island of Rhodes. The wreck lay 110 feet down and buried in the sand. What attracted divers' attention was a scattering of pieces of glass of many different colors poking through the sandy bottom. Later on in this project, whole bottles, pitchers, tumblers, and bowls were found as well as a half ton of collects (glass "ingots") which are the glassmakers raw material. Pieces of ship gear were found as well as some interesting pieces of pottery which one scholar identified as Islamic imitations of T'ang Dynasty pottery from China. Coins found nearby suggest that the ship was a 10th or 11th century trader from the Moslem world or possibly from Christian Bysantium.

5. A Dutch East India Company ship, The *Witte Leeuw* (White Lion) sunk in 1631 on its way back from the Spice Islands in the harbor of the island of St. Helena in the South Atlantic. The victim of Portuguese raiders, she was firing back when an explosion occurred on board, blowing her aft section to bits. None of the large shipment of diamonds listed on the ship's manifest was recovered. But in the 1970s a treasure in Chinese pottery of the kind often called Chinese export ware (cobalt blue design on white) was retrieved intact. It had been packed amid tons of pepper and other spices which proved to be excellent packing material.

6. In the late 1970s, a 14th century Chinese trading junk was found in the Yellow Sea, apparently sunk during a violent storm as it rounded the Southwest coast of Korea. Using the latest technology it

is being carefully evacuated. Already many exquisite pieces of Chinese pottery have been recovered, some crafted as early as the 13th and 14th centuries. These will be on view at the National Museum of Korea in Seoul. South Korean Navy scuba divers located more than 200,000 Chinese coins, the most recently minted were dated 1331, plus an additional 12,000 artifacts.

7. The December, 1979, *National Geographic* contained a report on two Spanish galleons sunk in 1724 off the North East coast of Hispaniola (Dominican Republic). They were named *Guadaloupe* and *Tolusa* and together they carried 1,200 passengers and crew and more than 400 tons of quicksilver and other assorted cargo. The mercury was a needed ingredient in the refining of gold and silver, done in the colonies before shipment to Spain. The ships had already made a provisioning stop in Puerto Rico and were headed for Havana and the final leg of their run to Vera Cruz when a hurricane struck. Only 40 to 50 feet down, the ships had been broken up against coral reefs. The quicksilver had dissipated into the sand but much other treasure was recovered which helped to fill in our picture of life in the Spanish colonies. One of the largest finds ever was of jewelry including magnificent pins, rings and bracelets with pearls, diamonds, rubys and emeralds set in gold or silver.

8. In 1981, Japanese divers found the wreckage of a Mongol fleet believe to be that of Khubilai Kahn. Twice in the thirteenth century the Mongols threatened to invade Japan. Their second attempt was foiled by what the Japanese call "the devine wind." All evidence so far indicates the fleet was dashed against the rocks of Tashema Island in a typhoon. Salvaging just began in 1981. Since Khubilai Kahn was attempting to invade with 40,000 troops in some 1,000 junks, salvaging operations could continue almost indefinitely.

9. In 1982, there was talk of locating two more recent wrecks—the *Titanic* which sunk in the North Atlantic in 1912, the victim of a collision with an iceberg, and the *Andria Doria* which sank about 25 years ago. In 1980 and 1981, a consortium of interests tried unsuccessfully to locate the *Titanic* which sunk in very deep water. The *Andria Doria* is only 250 feet down in a channel near New York harbor, but there are difficult currents. Divers have visited the site but have not figured out how to reach the purser's office which would contain a wealth of jewels and cash in its safe. In 1981 the expedition to the *Andria Doria* did recover one safe from the Bank of Rome which was located on the first class foyer, estimated to contain one million dollars in cash and jewelry. As this was written it was being kept in a salt water aquarium awaiting a television opening.

Advances in marine technology make it possible to locate additional wrecks and to work in deeper and deeper water. Almost nothing is technologically impossible in this new field, but costs are often prohibitively expensive.

Underwater archeology projects are most often financed by an assortment of grants from foundations, universities, governments and businesses. Despite the fact that such expeditions involve an increasing array of expensive scientific equipment, occasionally an individual or a group of individuals can attract sufficient investment capital to fund such a high risk project. The number of ancient ships being explored is increasing every year all over the world. Any increase in the number of available jobs is probably already being felt among the industries which manufacture the sophisticated equipment such as sonar, underwater cameras including TV cameras, transponders, divers' life support systems, etc.

The Job Outlook:

As a career objective, underwater archeology should be persued only by those for whom working at something exciting and fascinating is more important than making a lot of money. Although one occasionally reads about a treasure hunter who made a personal fortune, the chances of doing this are about as great as winning the Irish Sweepstakes.

Relatively few of the jobs relating most directly to underwater exploration are paid positions. These include the director, professional divers, persons who crew the boats and operate special equipment and a variety of other staff ranging from cooks to ship captains, sonar operators to television camera persons. The bulk of the "pick and shovel work" is done by students and other willing volunteers. Often cooperating museums or foundations which participate in projects contribute personnel. Universities may contribute the services of the director-professor or may only give a leave of absence.

Most of the paid personnel move into this field from other, ocean related areas. For example, a ship's captain or sailor on a ship engaged in underwater archeology may become so interested that he or she tries to limit other assignments to work in this exciting field. Professional divers may have served previously in the Navy or worked for a salvaging company or in rescue work. Persons new to the field may take additional training to learn to handle the delicate relics that are found.

There are two ways to become involved on a supervisory level. One is to earn a PhD and secure as a basic job a teaching position in a university with good department of archeology such as the University of Pennsylvania or University of Missouri. If a teacher has underwater archeology in mind he or she probably has already acquired diving skills and some know-how with small boats, or worked as a student volunteer on one or more projects as an adjunct to academic study degrees.

The other way is to have knowledge and interest in the field, and be rich. Such a person often already has the necessary skills in boating and diving, and is in a position to take part in archeological explorations by contributing their funding.

Some independent entrepreneurs have undertaken to raise funds for such expeditions, but only one has been consistently successful over many years and that is Jacques Cousteau who finances his explorations by making documentary movies.

Training

A number of colleges and universities offer a bachelor's and advanced degrees in archeology. These tend to concentrate on land based projects but a few are now including courses in underwater archeology.

Aquaculture—Farming the Seas

St. Peter's fish, so called because it is thought to be the kind of fish for which the apostle Peter, the Fisherman, fished the Sea of Galilee, may soon be grown on U.S. fish farms. More commonly known as the African Perch, it has always been a popular food fish in Africa, Asia, and the Middle East and is grown in large quantities in Israel. Only recently have U.S. culturists begun working with these fish. They are already being test-marketed in several states and getting good-to-excellent consumer acceptance. Major food chains are looking into the possibilities. Characteristics of the African Perch which make it easy to cultivate include its ability to stand crowding and poor water quality, its fast growth rate on a variety of low-cost natural organic materials, and the ease with which it propagates, especially in relatively warm water. Solar ponds under plastic airdomes, which use quantities of water heated during energy production, are being considered to provide just the right habitat. The hot water generated by power production is presently being returned to streams where it is causing ecologic problems because it is too warm.

The farming of fish and other seafoods, although a relatively new concept in the West, has been practiced for centuries in other parts of the world. Freshwater fish were being cultivated in China 3,000 years ago. The Romans grew some marine crops such as oysters.

However, as long as the oceans, lakes, and streams of the world abundantly provided fish and seafood, not much effort went into developing technology. But in the last few decades, a major effort to develop cultivation techniques has resulted in production of about six million metric tons, or 10% of the total world fish landings per year. Now that fish supplies are diminishing, and world population increasing, the time for scientific aquaculture has come!

Fresh Water Fish Culture

Although cultivation of marine species differs from cultivation of freshwater forms, sea farming owes much of its technology and promise to the freshwater culture industry. Historically, trout were the most important freshwater food fish cultured in the United States. Eggs were hatched and fry (recently hatched fish) raised in fish hatcheries first to re-stock the nation's lakes and streams for the pleasure of sportsmen. Bass has also long been cultured and released for the pleasure of sportsmen and commercial fishermen alike. This technology led to the understanding that artificial propagation can help to restore natural stocks, especially of estaurine spawners whose paths to spawning grounds have been blocked or whose nursery areas had been destroyed.[1]

Today, commercial trout culture is a multimillion dollar industry. Although it didn't exist 25 years ago, today, the cultured catfish industry produces at least 40,000 metric tons annually in 50,000 acres of ponds. This is two thirds of total U.S. fish aquaculture. The National Academy of Sciences estimated in 1970 that 250,000 metric tons per year of fish could be produced by 1985 and possibly a million metric tons per year by the year 2000.

Polyculture

One technique used with increasing effectiveness is polyculture, invented thousands of years ago by the Chinese for culturing freshwater Carp. Without any artificial manipulation, a given body of water is capable of sustaining only a limited number of any particular species. However, it may sustain additional fish of a different kind which do not compete with the first for the finite food supply. Similarly, if a third species, with still different food requirements, is

---

[1] Many species of salt water fish and shell fish return to bays and wetlands along the coast to breed in less salty water.

added to the pond, the total yield may far exceed that possible with two species. Polyculture is the growing of several species together to maximize utilization of food and water.

Salt Water Fish and Seafood Culture

Several kinds of fish and seafood require both fresh and salt water at various times in their life cycles. Two examples are salmon and prawns.

Recently, a net-cage-culture industry for salmon developed on the North American West Coast. Young fish produced in freshwater hatcheries are placed into floating pens in the ocean and fed artificially compounded rations. They grow rapidly to marketable size while protected from birds, fish, and other predators, including fishermen. Annual production has risen to over 1,000 tons in less than five years.

The Weyerhauser International Paper Company is also ranching salmon. Young salmon hatched on their fish ranches are returned to the open ocean. Three years later when the mature fish return, they are caught, the eggs removed, and the harvest sent to market. This is not yet a profitable operation since a percentage of those released are lost to commercial fishermen or ocean predators, but important improvements are being made in the technology of fish ranching.

As we know, salmon breed in freshwater. They sometimes fight their way many miles up-stream to lay their eggs in clear mountain streams. Many of those interested in increasing the world's food supply, and some entrepreneurial types are seeking a way to take advantage of this inborn trait of the salmon. They wonder what would happen if a large batch of hatchery produced salmon fry were released off the coast of South America or from islands in the South Atlantic. From there they would move with the currents in areas where there is much Antarctic krill. They would spend their lives happily growing fat by harvesting krill, that aboundant good food found in Antarctic waters which feeds everything from whales to penguins.

Since salmon are programmed by nature to return to their source to lay their eggs, they could then be trapped. Some imaginative inventers see them induced to swim right into the factory conveyor belts at floating or shore-based canneries.

A whole new industry—krill fishery—is in the process of being born. Since krill inhabit international oceans, the future of krill fishery is being shepherded by a welter of international organizations, both political and scientific. Leading is BIOMASS, the Biological Investigation of Marine Antarctic Systems and Stocks. Although a treaty which protects South Atlantic ecosystems is being drafted, about all the organizations involved now agree in is that much more must be learned about the nature of krill and their place in the eco-system in order to proceed.

Research is also increasing on the potential usefulness of algae—that most prolific of water plants and a plague to many fresh water lakes. It may someday be used in producing fertilizer, specialty chemicals and food supplements.

With enormous quantities of protein at stake, various plans for aquaculture will receive serious consideration in the years ahead. Here we run into the very same problems facing the companies preparing to mine the oceans. The fish are in international waters. Who would own them? The nations from which the fry were released and to which, presumably the adults would return? Or whomever caught them? How would the rest of the international family feel about the exploitation of this resource by a few maritime countries when many believe marine riches should benefit all including landlocked nations?

The life cycle pattern for the giant freshwater prawn, which may reach one-half pound or more, is the reverse to that of the salmon. Only the newly hatched larvae require salt water. After several weeks of developing in an estuary, they begin their journey up-stream.

The prawn farming industry is in its infancy. The prawn is a tropi-cal shell fish and must be grown under tropical conditions. Some pro-ducers have exploited artificially warmed water such as power efflu-ents, geothermal springs and solar greenhouses to produce prawns in cold climates. The National Fertilizer Development Center in North-west Alabama is testing the theory that prawns can become a profit-able cash crop for hog and poultry farmers. When placed in a warm pond, chicken or hog manure produces plankton—an algae like, micro-scopic animal which is a favorite food for shrimp and prawns and other kinds of fish. Plans are underway to use warmed waste water from Muscle Shoals to provide the needed tropical temperatures in winter. The Tennessee Valley Authority has a number of other fish farming operations using waste heat in the warm water left over from nuclear or steam generator plants.

At the current rate of expansion of the prawn-farming industry, this delicacy should begin appearing soon in luxury seafood markets, and within a few years in supermarkets.

The high popularity of shrimp in the U.S. has stimulated efforts to sea farm them. Some shrimp farms are in the sea or more correctly in estuaries, but many farms use ponds or even tanks on land. Modern shrimp farming required the development of hatchery techniques for large-scale production of fry or seed stock. It took nearly two decades to develop the technology. Today almost any quantity of seedling can be produced in captivity at almost any time of the year and almost anywhere. Some modern shrimp ponds produce thousands of pounds of shrimp per acre each year. The keys are the exclusion of predators, controlled stocking and feeding rates, and maintenance of good water quality. This contrasts with a harvest of a couple of hundred pounds per acre under good natural conditions. Such shrimp are very expensive but are already being successfully marketed. A shrimp farm on a desert in Mexico harvested over 65,000 shrimp in 1980 from one acre of water—more than a season's catch for a small fleet of boats.

In 1978, Hawaii took steps to help its aquaculture industry, putting more than one million dollars into research and development and its industry tripled by 1980. Today Hawaii has become the world's largest producer of freshwater prawns, and now exports tons of fish to Japan and the American mainland.

Commercial lobster culture is still in the research and development stage. Two problems are so far intractable. While a farmer may harvest his crop of shrimp from seed in less than six months, it takes a lobster several years to grow from birth to a weight of one pound. More difficult to solve, however, is the fact that no one has figured out how to restrain lobsters from their natural habit of cannibalism which, of course, would dissipate the crop.

Oysters, clams, and mussels can be and, in some parts of the world, are being grown. There are a few pioneering oyster farmers in Maine. One problem which slows up the development of vast culture industries is the shortage of seed. Just like any other farmer, an oyster farmer must plant seed if he is to harvest a crop and retrieving wild seed is an "iffy" business, since the success of natural reproduction fluctuates annually. Modern hatchery techniques are developing, and through carefully selecting breeding stock, are improving both the quality and size of the shellfish.

And there have been some beneficial local spin-offs as commercial aquaculture developed. Various groups around the U.S. are developing low-cost, solar-warmed fish culture ponds which can be used by homeowners or neighborhoods. Like the increasingly popular community garden movement, community ponds are designed to increase economic self sufficiency.

The principles of polyculture, when integrated with other processes are applicable to some of our other problems such as sewage treatment. Experimentation is going on as we increasingly recognize waste materials for the recoverable resources they really are.

The Job Picture

Except for experimental fish farms such as those mentioned above, most of the fish farming is done by independent farmers. At present fish farming accounts for only 3 or 4 percent of America's fish needs, but as these farms expand, they will come to resemble the factory farms which mass produce so much of our country's food. Fish farms are found in Mississippi, Tennessee, Kansas, Maine, Hawaii, the Northwest, in many of our estuaries and other places. Fish farming makes use of land which is less than ideal for standard crops.

In addition to an interest and knowledge in farming, a fish farmer must have a good knowledge of land management and must acquire a body of technology relating to the care, feeding, management, harvesting and marketing fish. So far, few agriculture departments in universities offer courses in fish farming. There is just one fledgling trade association of aquaculturists which is mentioned in the resources section. The long-range trend for an expanding number of jobs and careers in this field are most favorable.

Submersibles

There has been a rapid development over the past few years of all kinds of underwater craft, useful in advancing all aspects of the ocean industries discussed above. They range from especially pressurized diving suits, and mini-submarines for two, to underwater habitats which may accommodate several people for days or weeks.

People have been going under the sea in diving bells since the sixteenth century, but only a short distance down. A variety of manned craft, developed mainly by the Americans and the French, have been descending to deeper and deeper levels. In 1956, a diving saucer launched by Jaques-Yves Cousteau operated to 1,350 feet with a two-man crew. In 1965 Cousteau sent down *Conshelf Three*, a seafloor habitat which supported a six-man crew at 324 feet for 22 days. In 1966 two Americans took down *Techdiver PC 3B* to 600 feet off the coast of Spain looking for an H-bomb lost in the Mediterranean. The all time depth record was made in 1960 when the U.S. Navy's *Trieste* carried a crew of two down to the greatest ocean depth of 35,800 feet, more than six miles.

Because of special pressurized suits, individual divers can now operate today in depths to 2,000 feet. Several different submersible vessels are available which can operate at depths to 9,800 feet. The all-time work record for a submersible is probably held by the *Alvin*, which since 1964 has operated with a crew of three in waters to 13,000 feet, performing a variety of scientific tasks.

Submersibles represent a kind of tool developed for underwater research, and used throughout the ocean industries. They will play an increasing roll in ocean research and manufacturing. They can be used in repairing oil rigs, in locating nodules or repairing machinery for ocean mining, in deep-sea biological and geological research. They are expanding our knowledge about the planet we live on in many new directions.

Jobs With a Future

Aquaculturist	Marine transportation economist
Diver	Ocean farmer
Earthquake engineer	Ocean engineer
Fish farmer	Oceanographer
Geologist	Paleomagnetician
Geophysicist	Physical oceanographer
Inventer	Plate techtonics technician
Limnologist	Seafood culturist
Marine biologist	Shrimp/perch farmer
Marine ecologist	Tectonic technician
Marine geochemist	Underwater archeologist
Marine geologist	Volcanologist
Marine technologist	

For Further Information—Some starting points

Abel, Dr. Robert B., *Careers in Oceanography*, Sea Grant College Program, Texas A&M University, College Station, Texas 77843, 1979, free.

Advances in Aquaculture. New York: Unipub, 1979.

American Oceanic Organization, 777 14th Street, N.W., Suite 1014, Washington, D.C. 20005, (202) 638-4433.

American Petroleum Institute, 1801 K Street, N.W., Washington, D.C. 20006, (202) 457-7000.

American Society of Limnology and Oceanography, I.S.T. Building, Great Lakes Research Division of the University of Michigan, Ann Arbor, Michigan, (313) 764-2422.

Angel, M. V. and J. O'Brien (editors), *Progress in Oceanography* (an annual publication), Elmsford, N.Y.: Pergamon, 1982. Costs $100 but copies may be found in larger libraries.

Aquaculture Magazine, bi-monthly, features articles and advertising about production, processing, and marketing of finfish, shellfish, crustaceans, and aquatic plants, yearly buyers guide, Box 2451, Little Rock, Arkansas 72203. The May/June 1981 issue has a good coverage of fish farming.

Armstrong, John M. and Rymer, Peter C., *Ocean Management, a New Perspective*, Ann Arbor Science Publishers, Inc., The Butterworth Group, 1981.

Auikovchine, William and Richard Sternberg, *The World Ocean: An Introduction to Oceanography*, Englewood Cliffs: Prentice-Hall, 1981, second edition.

Costans, Jacques A. *Marine Sources of Energy*, Elmsford, N.Y.: Pergamon, 1980.

Dawes, Clinton J. *Marine Botany*, New York: Wiley-Interspace, 1981.

Kennett, James P. *Marine Geology*, Englewood Cliffs, N.J.: Prentice Hall, 1982.

Levinton, Jeffrey. *Marine Ecology*, Englewood Cliffs, N.J.: Prentice-Hall, 1982.

Limburg, Peter R. *Farming the Waters*. New York: Beaufort Books, 1981.

Marine Technology Society, 1730 M Street, N.W., Suite 412, Washington, D.C. 20036, (202) 659-3251.

National Ocean Industries Association, 1100 17th Street, N.W., Washington, D.C. 20036, (202) 785-5116.

New Alchemy Institute, 237 Hatchville Road, East Falmouth, Massachusetts 02366. This membership organization ($25.00 per year) serves as a trade association and provider of information for this fledgling aquaculture industry.

Oceanic Society, Stamford Marine Center, Magee Avenue, Stanford, Connecticut 06902, (202) 327-9786. The Society publishes *OCEANS* magazine.

The Oceans and You. Marine Technology Society, 1730 M Street, N.W., Suite 412, Washington, D.C. 20036. $3.00.

Opportunities in Oceanography. Smithsonian Press, Washington, D.C. 20560. $1.25.

Ross, Frank. *Jobs in Marine Science*. New York: Lathrop, Lee, and Shepard Books Division of William Morrow, 1974 (for children).

Scripps Institute of Oceanography, 8602 La Jolla Shores Drive, LaJolla, California 92093. The Public Affairs office may provide a list of colleges offering degree programs in oceanography and marine sciences.

Sea Technology Handbook Directory. Compass Publications, 1117 19th Street, North Arlington, Virginia 22209, 1982 (published annually). (703) 524-3136. Provides names and addresses for service, research, construction, and other firms in the marine science field. $18.50.

Scrutton, R. A. and M. Talwani. *The Ocean Floor*. New York: Wiley, 1982.

Sea Grant Today, a bi-monthly magazine. Extension Division, Virginia Polytechnic Institute and State University, Blacksbury, Virginia 20612, free.

Stickney, Robert R. *Principles of Warmwater Aquaculture.* New York: Wiley, 1979.

Training and Careers in Marine Science, International Oceanographic Foundation, 3979 Rockenbacker Causeway, Miami, Florida 44149. 50¢.

U.S. Department of Commerce, National Oceanic and Atmospheric Administration, 6016 Executive Boulevard, Rockville, Maryland 20852. N.O.A.H. Information: (301) 443-8243.

University Curricula in the Marine Sciences and Related Fields, Academic years 79 through 81; U.S. Department of Commerce, National Atmospheric and Oceanic Administration, Office of Sea Grant, 6010 Executive Boulevard, Rockville, Maryland 20852, 200 pages, free.

Wood, Jonathan. *Your Future in the Science of Oceanography.* New York: Rosen Press, 1982. $7.97.

Woods Hole Oceanographic Institution, Woods Hole, Massachusetts 02543.

Yung, C. Shang. *Aquaculture Economics: Basic Concepts and Methods of Analysis.* Boulder: Westview Press, 1981.

Chapter 11

SPACE TRANSPORTATION CAREERS

The conversation was about the Space Shuttle. "I know what a shuttle is," claimed one lively participant. "We have a shuttle bus in our neighborhood. It runs from Pendleton Street to the Subway Station and back every 15 minutes. But where are we supposed to shuttle to in space? And why?" The questions were good ones. To many people the space factories, solar power stations and space colonies to which the shuttle might go, look like so many impossible dreams.

The annals of human progress, however, always begin with an impossible dream. To sail around the world was the "impossible dream" of the 15th century. We have all read about the organizing and persuading that was necessary before this dream could begin to come true and it would not have been possible even then had not ship building and navigational technologies been advanced enough to carry it out. Many things had to come together—some economic, some political, and some technological before men like Columbus and Magellan could succeed.

So it is with exploring the frontiers of space today. As we approach the end of the 20th century, many things are coming together on which scientists have been working since the early 1920s. The Space Shuttle, which now seems to be a shuttle to nowhere, is to space exploration and development, what the sturdy sailing ships and accurate compasses were to the 15th century explorers. A future for industrial and commercial activities in space now look possible according to recent studies. Communications satellites (as yet the only economic success) will soon be joined by other types of satellites. Some of the newer satellites are instrumented to improve our capacity for studying the earth. Some will be used for energy production or for materials processing (such as for drugs or silicone chips) for eventual return to Earth. In effect, they will be sky laboratories or space factories. Collectively referred to as space industrialization, the economic viability of all of them depend upon the availability of a dependable space transportation system.

The significance of the development of a space transportation system has been compared to the development of the railroad in the late 1880s. While the pony express and the covered wagons were romantic, no major development of the West could take place until there was a dependable, regular way to get people, materials and products there and back. The successful launching and return of the first manned space flights is more like the first round trip of the newly built railroad to the West.

World's First Reusable Space Shuttle

In 1981, the Space Shuttle Columbia made its maiden voyage into orbit and returned safely. It was a first in the book of records of the achievements of mankind.

To get the Columbia into orbit required launching a combination package of the craft itself, a huge external fuel tank, and two solid rocket boosters. (One science writer thought it looked like the Taj Mahal.) Columbia's own mighty engines go into action at launch, drawing of fuel from the external tank. The two solid rocket boosters are needed in addition to lift the package through the thickest part of the atmosphere. This takes only two minutes—until the boosters have used up their fuel. They are then released and fall to earth, slowed and cushioned by a parachute. The shuttle and its external fuel tank continue toward orbit for another six minutes. At this time the fuel in the external tank has been about expended. Shuttle motors are turned off while the tank separates and begins to fall. In the case of the first shuttle flight, this happened over the Indian Ocean. The orbital navigation thrusters then go into operation to accurately insert the Columbia into the desired orbit.

The breakthrough in the case of the Columbia was not the launch but the return of the spacecraft. In all previous manned space flights only a small capsule containing the astronauts and instruments came back, and these fell in the ocean. But all of Columbia came back intact, landing with breathtaking precision on a desert runway at Edwards Air Force Base in California. The two solid booster rockets were recovered from the Atlantic Ocean. The cast-off external fuel tanks burned up on re-entry into the atmosphere. Perhaps at a later time a way will be found to make them reusable, or more likely usable for some purpose in space platform building.

Small and stubby when measured by modern jumbo jet standards, the Columbia is about the size of a DC-9. According to astronaut Michael Collins, it "looks like a cross between the Concorde and a Mack truck." But the pinnacles of technological advancement which it represents are many indeed. Here are just a few examples.

The Heat Shield System

The tiles which cover much of Columbia are composed of 90 percent air, 10 percent silica fibers, and a black glazed coating of borosilicate glass which dissipates about 95 percent of the heat. The interior silica fibers absorb the remaining 5 percent thus keeping the metal skin of Columbia from melting and burning up in the intense heat of re-entry.

The Motors

The Columbia's three motors are rocket combustion engines which run on liquid fuel. Once it is in space, two smaller engines are used to maneuver it into the correct orbit. These are also used to slow down just prior to re-entry when the craft is turned around so the motors can be used as a counter-thrust against their forward speed.

Columbia runs on a combination of liquid hydrogen and liquid oxygen. Scientists long ago learned that to get maximum thrust or efficiency from this fuel, it must be delivered for use at incredibly high pressures. They learned also that when you compress gases like oxygen and hydrogen to the point of liquification, it dramatically decreases their temperatures. The fuels loaded into the Space Shuttle and its auxiliary tanks just before a launch are so cold that serious icing problems might occur should the launch take place through a rain storm.

Many of the major challenges in developing space technology relate to handling extremes of heat and cold. As cited above, heat shield tiles now protect the craft from melting during the extreme heat of re-entry. But fueling and operation of the engines present a whole different range of heat-cold problems.

Even before scientists could liquify oxygen or hydrogen, they had to devise a method of containing them in liquid states. On the heels of solving this problem came the need to find ways to transport and load these super-cold fuels into tanks and to develop delivery systems within the engines which could take the fuel from the tanks to the combustion chamber.

Because this mixture of liquid hydrogen and oxygen burn at an incredibly high temperature—5500° F which far exceeds the melting point of steel, the combustion chamber and the nozzle must be continuously cooled. This is done by diverting a portion of the liquid hydrogen fuel to circulate around the combustion chamber and the nozzle which ultimately expels the super-heated gases. The hydrogen fuel used for cooling is further compressed to a pressure of 6,000 pounds per square inch by a remarkably small high pressure hydrogen turbopump built into the engine. The temperature of the circulating hydrogen is minus 423° F. This system manages to maintain metal temperatures at a relatively cool 1,000° F for the parts immediately surrounding the combustion chamber.

When one considers that ordinary metals melt at a far lower temperature than 5500°, and shatter into uselessness at temperatures as low as minus 423°, one can appreciate the magnitude of the scientific accomplishments the Space Shuttle represents.

We took time to mention only a few of the most spectacular technological achievements which made the space shuttle possible. Each one of these—the motors and the heat shield system—required the solution of hundreds of technical problems. This includes the development of a wide variety of new materials to assure the operation in extreme heat and extreme cold—in a vacuum of space or the air of our atmosphere. These advances were made in dozens of different sciences and industries all cooperating and focusing on the objective of developing a viable space transportation system.

Just as the first railroads borrowed their open coaches from the preexisting horse-drawn street car industry, so space transporation began with things we had learned for aviation. Many more challenges remain to be met. Materials need to be developed in the aerodynamics, astrophysics, and life support sciences before space shuttles can provide comfortable quarters for any lengthy travel in space.

Where to in Space?

After the construction of the first transcontinental railroad, there was a delay before there were any significant places to go and before there were people and goods to fill the trains to capacity. So it is in space. First come the dreams, then the vehicles, and finally plans for the industrialization of space.

According to a book, *Space Transportation Systems—1980–2000*, published by American Institute of Aeronautics and Astronautics, we are in the first of three stages of development in space transportation.

The first phase is to develop "Easy Access Into and Out of Space." This phase, which we are now beginning, includes the development of (1) space shuttle operations; (2) larger payloads capability; (3) low earth orbit space stations; (4) launching from shuttles of communications and other observational satellites into higher geosynchronous orbit. (That is an orbit at an altitude of 23,300 miles, at which height the orbital speed is synchronized with the earth's speed so that the satellite remains over a fixed location on earth.) (5) improved astronomical observational capacities; and (6) space rescue capabilities. The first phase is estimated to be completed by 1990.

The second phase is the development of "Permanent Occupancy on Near Earth Space," and includes development of (1) space manufacturing; (2) geosynchronous space stations; (3) orbital space facilities or platforms; (4) large structures applications (learning how to build and use them); (5) space base operations (bases for further construction and development of space colonies, factories, solar power stations, outer space exploration, etc.). This phase is estimated to be completed between 1995 and 2000. However, these target dates set some time ago are now considered "too optimistic" by an official of the National Space Institute.

The third phase which will probably not get into full swing until the early years of the next century is to develop "Limited Self Sufficiency in Space." This phase will include the further development of the stages just discussed plus probably (1) further exploration of extraterrestrial materials and energy sources; (2) a lunar base where raw materials may be mined; (3) space construction of industrial facilities, factories, processing plants, etc.; and (4) space colonies or habitats with closed ecology agricultural production and limited urban facilities for living and working; and (5) expansion of an inner or low earth orbit space transportation system between and among growing number of facilities, sort of a "space inter-urban transportation system."

All of these phases overlap, of course. Steps being taken right now pertain to all three phases. Just as the space program up until this point has provided much of the technology needed to develop the space shuttle, the operation of the space shuttle program will build the background of research and exploration needed to proceed with phases two and three.

Before we go too far out in space as the futurists see it, let us look at a few of the things you can expect before 1995—things which are laying a firm foundation for the later phases.

What We Are Doing To Fulfill Phase I

The Columbia's maiden voyage was also its first test flight in space. In addition to general operations into and out of space, the cargo bay doors—those huge, clam-like doors which cover more than half the length of the craft—were opened and found to work perfectly. Actually, the Shuttle cannot stay long in space with the doors closed. They must be opened to radiate waste heat. Had there been any hitch, Astronaut Crippen would have had to take a space walk to investigate how to get them closed again.

A second successful test flight for Columbia was made in November 1981. That trip carried some scientific payload in the form of a variety of earth-monitoring instruments. They are designed to do such things as map geological features with radar, locate and measure air pollution, and measure the distribution of vegetation on land and algae in the oceans. In addition, the huge manipulator arm or crane mounted at one end of the cargo bay was tested. Among other things, it is designed to maneuver later cargoes of satellites and their booster rockets out of the bay and into position to launch. Because of some minor difficulties, this mission was called home after only two days of the scheduled five. However, most of the scheduled tests will be completed successfully.

A third successful flight was made in March 1982. The fourth successful flight landed on July 4, 1982 after a final week of testing in space. Columbia will soon be joined by a sister ship, Challenger, which flew its first mission early in 1983. The third and fourth, Discovery and Atlantis, are scheduled for their first flights in 1984 and 1985. As each new shuttle comes on line and is tested, it will be placed in a regular schedule of flights to be used by the research scientists and industries of the world. The expectation is that by the end of this decade, the four orbiters could be making a total of about 50 flights a year. This was the target figure, but space officials' estimates now range as low as ten per year. These flights can vary in length from a few hours to a full week.

Work on increasing payloads goes on constantly. This is accomplished mainly by making any needed equipment smaller and lighter and also by improving the engines. Future generations of shuttles (those next models to be designed after the first four have been finished) will probably be larger than the DC-9 sized Columbia.

The earliest low Earth orbit space stations will be constructed from materials manufactured on Earth and carried aloft by the shuttles. Research is now developing materials, construction plans and methods. What needs to be tested in space will be evaluated on space shuttle missions. Due to limited capacity of the fuel cells which power the shuttle, it can only stay in orbit about seven days. The early development of power utilization stations is planned, making longer stays in orbit a reality. These could be free floating arrays of solar panels—sort of space electrical outlets—into which the shuttles could plug to recharge.

Columbia has already successfully launched communications satellites—a stage IV objective. Communications satellite launches make up a large part of the bookings for the first 68 shuttle flights running through the fall of 1986. Incidentally, the cost of a shuttle flight in 1981 dollars is about $35 million. Four relatively small satellites and their booster rockets can be launched from a shuttle flight for approximately $9 million. It is hard to project the cost of future space flights. Like everywhere else their costs will be subject to pressures exerted by inflation and the general health of our economy.

In 1985 NASA plans to launch and deploy a 45 foot long space telescope from a shuttle which will train five astronomical instruments on various regions of the universe. The space telescope can pick out objects 50 times fainter than those visible using earthbound telescopes. It will expand and deepen our look at the universe 350 fold. Also planned is the launch of a probe to Jupiter. Within the decade we should have a much expanded knowledge about the universe of which we are a part.

Plans are already being made to develop space rescue capacities so they will be available by the time shuttle flights go into regular operation. The prototype of the "rescue ball" is already in use by astronauts in training. It is big enough to hold one person and can be carried by a rescuing astronaut like a suitcase. It has a leak-proof, layered construction which withstands temperatures from minus 160° to plus 250° F.

What We are Doing To Fulfill Phases II and III

Early experiments in processing materials in space took place on some of the early space missions and particularly aboard Skylab. For $9 million or so depending on options, shuttle users can rent the new European-built Spacelab—a shirt-sleeve laboratory that fits into the cargo bay. The West German government has booked two Spacelab shuttle flights to experiment with processing materials in microgravity. McDonnell Douglass and Ortho Pharmaceuticals have reserved a Spacelab to test a way of extracting enzymes and hormones by using electrical fields to separate them from surrounding biological materials. If the experiment is successful, the two companies hope to put a commercial plant in orbit before the year 2000.

Giant corporations and governments are not the only potential users of the Spacelab or space shuttle flights. For $3,000 to $10,000 with only $500 down, any individual or group can send up a self-contained experiment weighing up to 200 pounds and occupying no more than 5 cubic feet. NASA has already sold hundreds of what they call "Getaway Specials." NASA hopes that by making these research capacities available to individual inventors or small companies, it may eventually reap a harvest of creative new ideas on manufacturing in space.

Everything that we have learned in the space program so far, plus everything we learn throughout the space shuttle program will combine to make possible the fulfillment of the third stage, but it is a little early to be specific. Space shuttles cannot fly up to the high orbits occupied by most communications satellites (23,300 miles high). Some envision a "space tug" fleet to cover these intermediate ranges to take service personnel to these satellites as needed. Futurists write about our plans for mining the moon and using the minerals to manufacture products in space. Other futurists wax poetic and build scale models of huge space colonies. While these may already be in the pipelines of scientific development, they will not offer much in the way of new careers before the year 2000.

The Job Outlook

All of the "right now" jobs which are closely involved with space travel are with the government's National Aeronautics and Space Administration. Between 1978 and March of 1981, NASA added 35 persons to its qualified astronauts roster. Nineteen more were in training. Some of these are women who now can be accepted for astronaut training providing they meet the same age and rigid physical and mental requirements. A German, a Dutch, and a Swiss scientist are being trained as astronauts to accompany Spacelab—built by a consortium of companies in member countries of the European Space Agency. An expansion of the shuttle program has led to specialization among astronauts. Now not all need to be pilots as was true in the beginning. While pilots will still fly the ship, as did Crippen and Young on Columbia's first flight, other specialists will tend to "space business." They will see to it that the satellite cargos are launched. They will walk in space as needed to tend scientific payloads exposed in open space. Specialists working within the Skylab may assist scientists from companies renting the Skylab. They also will attend to turning on or off switches of the "Getaway Specials" which are mainly self-contained packages.

Many more "right now" jobs are available in many private corporations. These include smaller companies which hold NASA contracts to build or furnish parts for NASA specified projects. At this point the greatest shortages are of very highly qualified scientists (training and experience beyond the PhD level). Depending on the focus of their interest, it should also be obvious that there are many jobs in the communications industry (radio and television), the computer-electronics industries, and in the energy industry (solar, development of new fuels, etc.) which also relate to the field of space transportation. As is the case in many of the other newest of the new industries, the future is widest open to those who are highly trained and highly skilled in more than one scientific area relating to problem solving in the space transportation area.

Marvin Robinson, Chief of the United Nations Outer Space Affairs Division, told *Forbes Magazine* (February 1982) that there have already been many benefits provided throughout the world as a result of our exploration of outer space. An international telecommunications satellite consortium, a system of 105 countries, does a $2 billion a year business. In many countries it is simpler to make an overseas call than to make a local call because this system works so well. In India, an instructional television network has been developed which reaches thousands of villagers by satellite. Better weather predictions result from daily weather satellite television pictures. These observational satellites also give geological, topological, and hydrological information. They can detect crop disease, locate and measure natural resources of many kinds.

The future development of outer space suffers from political problems similar to those relating to the oceans. The U.N. has been working on a treaty governing the use of remote satellites. Some countries feel they should be the first to get information about their country's resources received by remote sensing satellites, and that such information should not be made available to third parties without their prior consent. Third world countries, many of which have great resources, do not usually have access to satellites. They tend to feel that outer space is the common heritage of mankind, and that all should benefit as equally as possible from its development. Technologically developed countries feel that those who take the risks, provide the research and development, build the hardware, invest vast amounts of capital, should receive a greater proportion of the gains. Mr. Robinson neatly digested this question in his interview. "No country can afford not getting involved in space technology," because the benefits will be so vast and so abundant and there will be more than enough to go around.

This optimistic view is probably right for the long run, but in the early 1980s the space program, like many other programs, is experiencing cut-backs due to the poor economy which in turn has caused a lessening of public enthusiasm. The two remaining shuttles of the first series known as the first generation, will be completed. Follow-up programs to develop the second generation (which will be improved on the basis of what we have learned through developing the first) have not yet been forthcoming. At the moment the program seems to be on "hold" which will further delay progress in space development. At latest report, however, NASA is still hiring some people and also issues career materials to help introduce youth and adults to NASA careers.

Meanwhile, hundreds, possibly thousands of jobs have already been created in electronics manufacturing of spin-off items which would never have been developed at all if it were not for the space program.

Jobs With A Future

Aerospace engineer
Astronaut
Astrophysicist
Celestial mechanics scientist
Ceramic engineer
Electron difrictionist
Exotic welder
Inverter (space systems)
Ionospheric plasmo physicist
Lunar miner
Lunar technician
Neutrino astronomist
Operations researcher and systems management specialist
Planetary geologist
Planetary scientist
Radio astronaut
Radiographer
Selenologist
Spacecraft controller
Space colonist
Space mechanic
Space physicist

Note: Most of the fields covered in this book employ technical writers and forensic scientists. They handle the communications aspects of these businesses and industries. Forensic scientists are usually fully trained in their chosen scientific fields. They often have many years of experience in research and development. What they do is to handle the communications and legal-argumentative aspects of their fields. For example, a forensic scientist in the atomic energy field would be skilled in handling all the issues and arguments which are constantly arising in that field. Likewise, technical writers must understand the most complex of scientific subjects and processes, as well as the issues and arguments. Clearly this requires more education and background in the scientific field itself than most ordinary writers possess. Like many other careers with a future, these require a combination of scientific training and/or experience, plus well developed writing and oral communications skills.

For Further Information—Some starting points

Adelman, Andrew and Peter M. Biainum (editors). *International Space: Technical Applications.* San Diego, Univelt, Inc., 1981.

American Astronautical Society, 6060 Duke Street, Alexandria, Virginia 22304, (703) 751-7323. Its membership directory lists some 700 researchers and administrators in this area.

American Institute of Aeronautics and Astronautics, 1290 Avenue of the Americas, New York, N.Y. 10019, (212) 681-4300.

Chicago Society for Space Settlement, 4 N. Walker Drive, Addison, Illinois 60101, (312) 529-1049.

Clarke, Arthur C. *Challenge of the Spaceship.* New York: Pilot Books, 1980. $2.50.

The Directory of Aviation and Space Education, third edition, 1980-81; American Society for Aerospace Education, 1750 Pennsylvania Avenue, N.W., Suite 1303, Washington, D.C. 20006, (202) 347-5187. This is a membership publication which costs $35.00 for non-member. However, a membership application with yearly dues of $15.00 will bring you a copy of this directory.

Heppenheimer, T. A. *Colonies in Space.* Harrisburg: Stackpole Books, 1977.

Holmquist, R. (editor). *Life Sciences and Space Research.* Elmsford, N.Y.: Pergamon Books, 1979.

L-5 Society, 1620 N. Park Street, Tucson, Arizona 85719, (602) 522-6351. The Society is concerned with permanent space stations, advanced transportation systems, and eventual space colonies.

Morgenthaler, G. W. and M. Holstein (editors). *Space Shuttle and Spacelab Utilization: Near-Term and Long-Term Benefits for Mankind.* San Diego: Univelt, Inc., 1978.

O'Leary, Brian, *The Fertile Stars, Man's Look At Space as the New Source of Food and Energy,* New York: Everest House, 1981.

Ramo, Simon et al. *Peacetime Uses of Outer Space.* Westport, Ct: Greenwood, 1977.

Space Cadets of America, 256 S. Robertson Blvd., Beverly Hills, California 90211, (213) 273-6365. This group encourages interest in space related careers.

Space Enhancing Technological Leadership, edited by Lawrence P. Green. An American Astronautical Society Publication, Univelt, Inc., P.O. Box 28130, San Diego, California 92128, 1981.

The Space Enterprise, G. Harry Stine. New York: Ace Books (A Grosset and Dunlap Company), 1980.

Space Industries Society, 1627 Spruce Street, Philadelphia, Pennsylvania 19103, (215) 732-3306.

Stine, G. Harry, *Space Power*. New York: Ace Books, 1981.

Stockton, William and John Noble Wilford, *The New York Times Report on the Columbia Voyager Space Liner*. New York: Times Books, 1981.

Walker, Lawrence C. *The Exploration and Colonization of Space: Lessons From History*. Center for Education and Research in Free Enterprise. Texas A and M University, College Station, Texas 77843, 1980. $1.00.

Zimmerman, Howard. *Spaceships*. New York: Starlog Press, 1980. $7.95.

Chapter 12

FINDING YOUR WAY TO TOMORROW'S CAREER

Career decisions are among the most difficult choices we make in our life span. Whether it's your first position out of school or a mid life change in career fields, the decision involves a sequence of choices and challenges. A determination to start a new job or career presents challenges. You must obtain needed education or training, arrange to pay for it, and locate a suitable position.

It is surprising, but true, that despite the problems involved, the name of the game today is often "changing your career." Many young people just out of college are finding that the training they received is not appropriate for the jobs that are available. Older people see their current fields becoming obsolete because of technological advances and they must seek new ways to earn a living. In the early Reagan years changes in political philosophy plus vast government spending cuts displaced thousands of government workers. For many, their skills were not directly applicable in the private sector. Advances in technology, those described in this book among them, are obsoleting countless other jobs in the private sector almost daily.

How do you approach making a decision about a new career? What do you need to know about yourself, about the new field and its demands, about how you can pull it all together? Let's look at major considerations faced by everyone considering a job or career change. They fall into three general categories: Self knowledge, Career Research and Planning, Professional Guidance.

Self Knowledge

Matching people, their special talents, and desires to the most appropriate jobs has become highly specialized. Professional career guidance counselors, job placement specialists, and now a few professional psychologists address these problems. One thing they nearly all agree on is that finding the right job or career is highly personalized. Ask ten people you believe are happy in their work, how they got into it in the first place, and you will probably get ten different stories. Often the stories involve accidental meetings, sudden changes of personnel which put the person in the right place at the right time, or work accepted temporarily and in desperation, which developed into a lifetime interest. Their experiences are usually not replicable, nor are they of much help in guiding other seekers.

Another discovery is that those most successful in finding the very best places in the world of work—we mean careers which meet their needs and desires most completely—are those who understand themselves in depth. It is often helpful to compile on paper your own personal survey of needs, desires, and expectations, along with your own assessment of your talents, interests, and abilities. We suggest the following as a good start:

1. List your goals in life. What is most important to you? Divide this list into short and long-term goals.

2. List the subjects that interest you enough so that you have read quite a lot about them. Put a check mark (√) after any in which you have skills or have received education or training. Be sure to include any that seem "just natural" for you. For example, some people have a way with figures, or colors, or harmony, or words or whatever.

3. List your talents. What are you good at? Don't worry about overlap with your list of interests. We usually become interested in what we are naturally good at. List both esoteric and practical skills from skiing, macrame or painting watercolors, to drafting, typing, or cooking. Put a check mark (√) after any skill which is marketable whether or not you would ever want to make your living at it. Jot down as many as you can. More than one scientist has put himself through college by playing with a dance band. Secretarial, administrative, computer, and other skills can also be used to earn while preparing for a new career.

4. Assess your human relations skills and preferences. Also evaluate your communication skills. Do you like people? In large groups? Or small? Do you like to work with people? Do you like work which involves helping people? Do you prefer to work with a team, or as a loner? Can you persuade others to go along with you? Do you enjoy arguing? Winning arguments? Are you a good listener? In your ideal job, what percentage of your time would be used in working with people, with things, and with ideas?

5. Define the work environment you like best. Is it indoors, out-

doors, or both? Does it involve heavy machinery? Office equipment? Do you see yourself working at a desk? In a laboratory? A
production environment? Or the seas? In the air? In a moving vehicle? Or what?

6. List geographic factors, if applicable. To what other parts of
the country or the world would you be willing to go in order to pur-
sue your career objectives? Where are you currently unwilling to move?

It is also helpful to check out your personal habits of working and
thinking. Clear out any potential stumbling blocks to making a progressive career move. Consider the significance of the following char-
acter traits:

1. Indecisiveness: Are you a procrastinator? Most of us are at
times. Procrastination is a deadly enemy of decision making. Many
people procrastinate by going over the same territory in their thinking that they have been over before—in short, stewing around. This is
usually done in order to avoid the decision to which your previous
thinking led you. It may be a painful decision. You find yourself
thinking "There must be some other way!" In an effort to find one,
you keep repeating the same thinking. Try to catch yourself when
you begin to do this. Not only is it a waste of time, but it leaves the
problem unsolved. If you find yourself stewing around, you need to
ask yourself "Why am I avoiding this decision? Is it because I don't
like the decision to which my thinking has led me? Is it because I
honestly don't have enough information?" If this is the case, you
need to decide whether the needed information can be obtained
without too much delay. If not, ask yourself "Can I make this decision on the basis of the available facts, plus a calculated risk?"

2. Decisiveness: For many, the only advice received about decision making from parents, counselors, or teachers is that good decisions are based on facts. "Find out all you can about a particular
situation before you decide," they say. Essentially this is the scientific approach.

It is important to realize that most of the thinking in the scientific,
as well as the non-scientific world is not that logical. Certainly most
of the thinking which has gone on in the world has not been based
on logic. Respected leaders of the Roman world made political
decisions based on what their mentors gleaned from observing the
configuration of the entrails of a slain chicken. The Aztecs felt that
the Gods were angry with them when the earth shook or volcanos
erupted. "Wrong assumptions of cause and effect," we may think
smugly, but are we all that sure that we are operating on the correct
assumptions for today? Students of thinking would say that it is not

so much a question of right or wrong but that the Romans operated on a different system of thinking, using different basic assumptions. Roman soothsayers and their followers were *assuming* that there is a connection between the configuration of the entrails of a chicken killed on a certain day, and future events. The Romans believed a certain magic enabled soothsayers to derive wisdom that way. Today, we *assume* there is no connection. We do not believe in that kind of magic. Neither the Romans or anyone else ever proved it one way or the other.

The scientific method, which is our model for thought, grew out of the elaborate systems of logical thinking worked out by the Greeks. The scientific method adds a requirement that both the major and minor premices should be supported by much verifiable, concrete evidence before a conclusion can be drawn. Still, there is not much difference in the way we think and the way the Greeks thought some 2000 years ago. Our insistence on more concrete evidence has made the major differences in our ways of thought. In the example of the Aztecs given above, it has now been proved scientifically that volcanic eruptions and earthquakes are not caused by the anger of the Gods.

However, the vast majority of assumptions on which we base our thinking today, just as in ancient times, are not yet amenable to scientific proof. It is a shattering concept for some to realize that all chains of reasoning, whether they be scientific or not, rest on commonly accepted often unproved and unprovable basic assumptions. For a society to continue to operate its basic assumptions do not have to be proven or provable. They do have to be commonly accepted. Many of the world's conflicts can be traced to different commonly accepted basic assumptions held by the conflicting groups. Changes in commonly accepted assumptions occur very, very slowly, but they do occur. Perhaps some citizen of the world in the year 2500 will look with patronizing superiority at the ways we have attributed causes and effects, just as we now look back on the Romans and the Aztecs.

What does all this have to do with the average man or woman confronted with career decisions? If you are considering a career change you may confront innumerable educational challenges, indifferent potential employers, and often unpleasant employment settings.

It is helpful to recognize that all the people you meet may not operate on the same thought pattern you do. When you can recognize differences, you can better control the situation.

One must also recognize that emotions influence our thinking. The emotions themselves are in part the product of our psychological and physiological conditions of the moment. As one person put it, "Don't get carried away with your hopes, your dreams—or your fears." You can become more aware of the many factors that influence decision making both internally and externally.

3. Creative imagination: Let your creative imagination loose. Spend a little time daydreaming. For example, suppose you can imagine yourself to be an ocean mining engineer. You would be organizing and directing a fleet of complex mining and research vessels—solving problems—getting results! Good! People rarely achieve anything they never dreamed about first. Use your creative imagination in this way. Allow your mind to follow through with any of the areas which interest you.

4. Idle daydreaming: Idle daydreaming, however, is often a means of escaping the tedium of today's tasks. It is not creative! It does not move you one whit closer to the object of your daydream. Use it sparingly and with awareness.

5. Laziness: Everyone needs to honestly check his or her laziness quotient once in a while. If you are considering changing careers, you can look forward to a period of extra hard work in order to accomplish your goals. Honestly appraise your willingness to work. Compute the extra time it will take to set up the new career situation while maintaining yourself in your present work. Are you willing to make the necessary sacrifice? Are you enthusiastic about it? Or are you lukewarm?

Career Research and Planning

This stage is often carried on along with your self analysis. Both research and planning may be difficult and time-consuming. If you can find the right career guidance counselor, this person may be of great help in your transition.

1. Career Information Research: As you can tell from the previous chapters, the number and kinds of jobs is expanding so fast that it is not easy to learn about some of the newer ones. The obvious place to start is by following up on any of the relevant suggestions contained in the resources section at the end of chapters which particularly interested you. The publications and organizations listed there are starting points—that is, each can lead to further information sources.

Librarians in your community may help guide you to information within and beyond your local library. If you live near a college or university, check its library. Also, most schools have placement facilities and services. Check to see what information facilities they have that you may be able to use.

2. Make flexible plans: Careful planning is usually necessary if we are to reach any of our goals in life. This is true whether the goal is a leisurely automobile trip across the country, or a move from your present job to an entirely different type of work. As every planner has different needs, aspirations, and objectives, it is difficult to speak generally about planning. Your career plan will be similar to plans for that automobile trip. Both have a time frame and various stages and intermediate goals before the final objective. This can all be anticipated by your plans. As you move along, there may be many revisions. Some successful planners always include a contingency plan to be followed if the first one goes awry. Much of the information jotted down in your self-knowledge survey will be useful during this planning process.

3. *Seek professional help if needed*: Today's world is so fast moving and complex that it is little wonder finding a job or starting a new career is complicated and time consuming. Many persons making career changes have been helped by professional career guidance experts. A counselor can help with all three stages we have discussed above.

If you suspect that you have hidden talents or want to confirm an aptitude, counselors are trained to administer professionally devised tests and interest inventories. They also make good listeners if you wish to discuss your hopes and plans. They can provide expert advice.

Guidance counselors usually maintain a considerable collection of career information materials which they may give or loan you. They can help you find out where to obtain other needed facts. They are also familiar with training programs, and can assist you in entering the right educational preparation.

Counselors can also help with the actual job-hunting stage—advising on such key areas as your resume, job application, and interview techniques.

Finding the best career guidance counselor for you can be as tricky as finding the right professional in any area of personal service. Much depends on who is available where you are located. Here are a few suggestions.

1. Check local universties' guidance and placement services. If you are taking courses there you may be eligible for their personnel services. If not, sometimes you can make other independent arrangements. They can suggest community sources which might help.

2. Check with your local board of education. A network of career guidance counselors is associated with the public schools and a call to the supervisor of guidance may help you to find an independent counselor.

3. If you feel you can reveal your intentions to ultimately move to a new career, check with the personnel department of your present employer. Some enlightened organizations assist persons who wish to transfer to new areas.

4. Check the yellow pages of your phone book under the classification "vocational guidance." There are many specialists helping people find new careers. Most offer career guidance and testing services of various kinds. Some may also be listed under "employment agencies." A word of caution is in order. Many of the independent agencies are very professional and offer very helpful services. However, occasionally there is one which requires you to sign a contract for a lengthy series of tests and advisory services which you may not need. Check with other professional guidance personnel, or write the groups cited next.

5. The National Vocational Guidance Association, a division of the American Personnel and Guidance Association (APGA), is the professional association for career guidance counselors. Its address is: 2 Skyline Place, Suite 400, 5203 Leesburg Pike, Falls Church, Virginia 22041. It may be able to help you locate a vocational guidance counselor in your area.

6. The International Association of Counseling Services (an affiliate of APGA) lists approved counseling agencies all over the United States. Its address is: 5203 Leesburg Pike, Falls Church, Virginia 22041.

One point which has been stressed throughout this book needs reemphasis. In order to move to the top in any of these new areas, you usually need knowledge and skills in more than one field. Some move into new areas by adding computer skills to an area of expertise they already have such as engineering, health, or statistics. Others combine three areas such as computers, medicine, and communications. In your planning, analyze how you could use your present skills in combination with new skills or knowledge which have yet to be learned. Many of the most needed combinations are unique. Study the help-wanted ad sections in the *New York Times* (its semi-annually career supplement could be most helpful) or in other leading newspaper such as the *Wall Street Journal*. Trips to the library to study the help-wanted and job openings ads in professional and trade journals may also be most revealing.

Finding a Job or Career in Tomorrow's World

Today there are over 50 different ways to get a job or seek the career of your choice. Five years from now there will probably be even more ways, as the world grows more complicated. Those who find just the right jobs have usually used a number of methods. All things being equal, the more job seeking techniques used, the better your chances of locating a truly appropriate position. The following ways can be used. They are not listed in any order of priority.

1. Newspaper—place or answer an ad in a newspaper.[1]
2. Magazine—place or answer an ad in a periodical.
3. Read the Professional and Trade Association Job Finder[1]
4. Job banks—use services which list candidates for jobs.
5. Job registries—this is another form of a job bank.
6. Clearinghouse of jobs—use employment services which list candidates and vacancies.
7. Clearinghouse of jobs—use employment services set up in conjunction with national or regional meetings of professional organizations.
8. Cold canvas in person—call on employers, hope to find one with a vacancy appropriate for your skills and interests.
9. Cold canvas by telephone—call employers to identify organizations with appropriate vacancies.
10. Union hiring hall—use employment services set up by labor organizations.
11. Alumni office contacts—high school or college alumni offices may suggest former students in a position to help you.
12. Public career and counseling services—use state employment and other public career-oriented services.
13. Private career and counseling services—the fees charged by these organizations may be more than justified by the job search time saved.
14. Employment agencies—These may charge a fee or a percentage commission but only if you take a job through them.

---

[1] Two other books by Feingold may help. The first (with Glenda Ann Hansard-Winkler) is *900,000 Plus Jobs Annually: Published Sources of Employment Information*, cites hundreds of magazines which contain want ads for open positions. It is available for $9.95 from the Garrett Park Press, Garrett Park, Maryland 20896. The other (with Avis Nicholson) is the *Professional Trade Association Job Finder*, which lists employment-related activities of national and regional associations. It is also available from the Garrett Park Press.

15. Executive search firms—These are "head hunter" organizations retained by employers to identify persons for specialized jobs.
16. Volunteer work—millions have begun their careers by first gaining experience or a "foot in the door" through unpaid work.
17. Part-time work experience—A part-time job may be easier to obtain than full-time and may lead to a permanent position.
18. Temporary or summer work—These provide experience and an introduction to the employer's organization.
19. Make your own job—Free lance work may lead to self-employment or a job with an employer.
20. Join a 40 plus group—Most cities have these job clubs which specialize in older workers.
21. Join a 65 plus group—These organizations provide jobs and other services for senior citizens.
22. Join a job search club—Sharing job hunting experiences can provide new ideas and psychological support.
23. Tell friends and acquaintances—Most studies show that friends and family are the best single source of job leads.
24. Federal job centers—These offices, located in major cities, are a good source of job leads. Look them up in the telephone book under "U.S. Government."
25. Computerized placement services—Many organizations inventory candidates and employers by computers, to make job matches.
26. Social agency placement services—Along with social services, many of these groups now provide job counseling and placement assistance.
27. Membership services—Many professional and other organizations maintain employment assistance programs to aid their members.
28. Mail order job campaign—Send out dozens or hundreds of letters to potential employers, hoping to identify suitable openings.
29. School or college placement services—Both current students and alumni generally are eligible for help from these groups.
30. Association placement services—Many professional and other organizations include employment assistance as a part of their service program.
31. Trade placement services—In many occupations, an organized placement program operates.
32. Professional placement services—Use professional career place-

ment specialists, particularly if seeking a high level job.

33. Hotlines—Use these answering services (many operate 24 hours a day) maintained by community organizations or libraries.

34. Federal civil service offices—Contact employment offices of federal agencies in your area of interest.

35. State merit service offices—get in touch with appropriate state government agencies.

36. County or city personnel office—File for suitable openings with agencies of local government.

37. Internships—Use a paid or unpaid, short-term internship to gain experience and make contact with potential employers.

38. Work study program—Use a cooperative work-study program to gain experience and to make contacts in field of prime interest.

39. Networking—Expand contacts, which may help you, by working with peers, supervisors, friends, and others.

40. Use a mentor—Often older, more experienced persons to whom you turn for advice may take a special interest in your proper placement.

41. TV job and career announcements—Don't overlook ads placed on TV for employees.

42. Radio job and career announcements—Many employers, with numerous jobs, use radio to help solicit candidates for them.

43. Bulletin board posting—Check ads placed on career-related bulletin boards.

44. Check the *College Placement Annual*[2]

45. Check in-house job vacancies—Most progressive employers now post all vacancies for their current employers to examine and, if interested, apply for. This permits maximum use of upward mobility techniques.

46. DVR job placement services—Most state divisions of rehabilitation services offer disabled persons extensive job counseling and placement services.

47. Former employers—Don't hesitate to ask former employers for help.

48. Fellow employees—Persons who work with you might know of suitable vacancies in other offices or organizations.

49. Personnel office counseling—Many times, the personnel office

---

[2] The *College Placement Annual* is published by the College Placement Council, P.O. Box 2263, Bethleham, Pa. 18001 and lists hundreds of employers seeking to recruit college-trained persons. Copies are found in most college placement offices.

will counsel with you about career paths or alternative jobs in your organization.

50. Religious leaders—Often, ministers, rabbis, or priests know of potential employers, from among their members.

51. Library resources—Check Moody's Industrials, the Fortune "500 list" and other library reference books for employment suggestions.

52. Overseas work—Major religious groups and other international agencies may hire for jobs in other countries.

53. Sponsored interviews—If possible, have persons you know set up employment contacts for you.

54. Military services—Enlistment in one of the armed forces may provide both an immediate salary and job training in fields of interest.

For Further Information—Some starting points

Alexander, Sue *Finding Your First Job.* New York: E. P. Dutton, 1980.

Azibo, Moni and Therese Crylen Unumb. *The Mature Woman's Back to Work Book.* Chicago: Contemporary Books, 1980.

Barlow, Lawrence E. *How to Sell Yourself: The Job Seeker's Bible.* Lakeside, California: Vocational and Career Assessment, 1981.

Bolles, Richard N. *What Color is Your Parachute?* Berkeley: Ten Speed Press, 1982.

Catalyst Staff. *What to Do with the Rest of Your Life.* New York: Simon and Schuster, 1980.

Crane, Ruth and Marcine H. Goard. *Self-Evaluation Career Guide.* New York: Pilot Books, 1979.

Dauw, Dean C. *Up Your Career.* Prospect Heights, Illinois: Waveland Press, 1980.

Doss, Martha Merrill. *The Directory of Special Opportunities for Women.* Garret Park, Maryland: Garret Park Press, 1981.

Figler, Howard. *The Complete Job Search Handbook.* New York: Holt, Rinehart, and Winston, 1979.

Gaymer, Rosemary. *Teach Yourself How to Find a Job.* Toronto: University and College Placement Association, 1980.

Ginn, Robert J. Jr. *The College Graduate's Career Guide.* New York: Charles Scribner's, 1981.

Hecht, Miriam and Lillian Traub. *Dropping Back In.* New York: Dutton, 1982.

Jackson, Tom. *The Perfect Resume.* Garden City, N.Y.: Anchor Press, 1981.

Kocher, Eric. *International Jobs—Where They Are, How to Get Them.* Reading, Mass.: Addison-Wesley, 1979.

Krannich, Caryl Rae. *Interviewing for Success.* Virginia Beach, Virginia: Impact Publications, 1982.

Mitchell, Joyce Slayton. *I Can Be Anything—Careers and Colleges for Young Women.* New York: College Board Publications, 1978.

Nutter, Carolyn F. *The Resume Workbook.* Cranston, RI: Carroll Press, 1978.

Rinella, Richard J. and Claire C. Robbins. *Career Power.* New York: Amacom, 1980.

Rust, H. Lee. *Job Search: The Complete Manual for Job Seekers.* New York: Amacom, 1979.

Schmidt, Peggy J. *Making It on Your First Job.* New York: Avon Books, 1981.

Souerwine, Andrew H. *Career Strategies: Planning for Personal Achievement.* New York: Amacom, 1978.

Summers, Jean. *What Every Woman Needs to Know to Find a Job in Today's Tough Job Market.* New York: Fawcett Publications, 1980.

Teich, Albert H. (editor). *Technology and Man's Future.* New York: St. Martin's Press, 1981.

Villaldo, Alberto and Ken Dychtald (editors). *Millennium: Glimpses into the 21st Century.* Los Angeles: J. P. Tarcher, 1981.

Waelde, David E. *How to Get a Federal Civil Service Job and Avoid a RIF.* Washington: Fedhelp Publications, 1982.

Zehring, John William. *Careers in State and Local Government.* Garrett Park, Maryland: Garrett Park Press, 1980.

IN CONCLUSION

"The past is gone. The present is lost as it arrives. There is only the future," as the Introduction pointed out. In Chapter 1, "The Future as the Experts See It," futurists sketched a broad and exciting picture of the world of tomorrow. On this stage will be played out the new careers described in this book, as well as many others which will be covered in future volumes in this series.

"The future belongs to those who prepare for it." While not new, this observation certainly applies to times like ours. Nowhere is our current rate of change, or need to understand and adjust to the future more apparent than in the world of work. New jobs, new careers, new concepts of work are affecting the new world in which we will live and work. In selecting careers from the new areas covered in this book, we enter fields developed directly from new technology which led to entirely new industries.

Had this book been begun even one year from now, it would have included a chapter on fiber-optics and lasers, two related fields of the future which have not yet become industries. Fiber-optics technology is based on the transmission of light through slender strands of ultra-pure glass or plastics. Fiber-optics is already being used for much diverse purposes as decorative lighting, long distance communications, and for the precise diagnostic tools used by physicians, jet engine inspectors, and atomic reactor inspectors. Bell Laboratories is busy researching and developing many new uses.

The Bell System recently began installing the world's largest laser-powered telecommunications system. The 611-mile system, which will link phones in the Washington, Philadelphia, New York, and Boston metropolitan areas, should enter service in 1984. "We're entering the age of *photonics*—carrying communications on pulses of light, rather than as electrical signals," says Richard Jacobsen, Vice President of American Telephone and Telegraph's Company's Long Lines Department. "Eventually, lightwave communications may offer a high-quality, low-cost way to bring a variety of improved voice, data and video services to customers in offices, shops, and homes."

Twenty laser beams were used in an experiment at Lawrence Livermore Laboratories in California. Using "laser pellets" they sought to control nuclear implosion so that fusion can become a useful source of energy. New laser weapons, similar to the zap guns of "Star Wars" are on the drawing boards. Lasers are being used in weather observations to measure wind speed and air column turbulance. Laser surgery, specifically eye surgery, which calls for an unusual degree of precision, is already being practiced at The Eye Institute of Boston. It has proven highly useful in attaching detached retinas.

This is not to say that these, and other emerging industries do not have roots in the past. We also are not implying that all skills developed in past or current jobs are to be obsoleted with the coming new industries. There is a continuity to life which cannot be broken if civilization is to go on. All civilizations from the most primative days have had some form of communications. For example, what's new about the information industry which is on the cutting edge of communications at this time, is the rising importance of information handling, collection, storage, recall, and transfer. As one of the futurists put it earlier, information is rapidly becoming the very basis of our society. More than 80% of those employed in the U.S. will be in the communication industry by the year 2000. But its roots go back as far as the first exchange of messages between primative peoples.

Computers have their roots in the 19th century. Robotics an offspring of the computer industry, is becoming an increasing reality. The age-old dream of creating mechanical men to do our bidding and our work is coming true. Robots are taking routine, repetitive jobs from humans, liberating them for better jobs. Robot psychologists and robot tutors are not too far away.

Our energy industry has existed, as it is now, only since the 18th century. In the 1700s society developed new energy industries using water, wind, and coal. Today we are on the threshold of an era of solar energy—the direct conversion of sunlight, wind, tidal, or geothermal energy into electric power. Our traditional sources of energy from fossil fuels are now becoming too expensive to exploit. There has been a heartening explosion of responses to solving the international energy problem which has resulted in many new jobs.

Ocean travel and fishing have always existed, but the new ocean industries may provide our next most unique step forward in human progress. While developments which are making possible space travel, space living, other planet mining, and space manufacturing, will take us across yet another threshold.

Because there are so many exciting developments in traditional industries, and ways of making a living, as well as in these entirely new areas, a second, third and fourth volumes are contemplated for this series.

A second volume is planned to cover the new developments in customary industries, like agriculture, communications (radio, TV, telephone), entertainment, professional sports, the arts, recreation, and entrepreneurship.

Volume three will concern the latest developments in the service industry. This broadened concept of services not only includes the usual household, repair, personal (health and legal), and social services, but also the provision of expertise and the selling of advice and information of all kinds. This reflects the shift from industrial society where we make things for one another, to the service society, where we provide all kinds of information and services for one another.

Another area where extensive changes are underway is in medicine where new and exciting breakthroughs are announced almost daily. However, revolutionary changes are also underway in the familiar professions of engineering, teaching, and law. The new jobs in what we call the traditional disciplines resulting from technological and scientific advances will be the subject of a fourth volume.

The importance of preparatory training in more than one field has been stressed repeatedly in this book. The era just ahead, the era into which we are now rushing, will demand the flexibility of a generalist as well as the expert knowledge of the specialist. The people who will do best in the coming days will have skills in several areas. They also will have those personal abilities needed to work as members of a team which together can focus a wide variety of experience, backgrounds, and knowledge on a single problem.

Each generation's activity and achievements work to change the educational and training requirements for the following generation. Each new generation faces greater, more complex, more difficult challenges then the one which preceded it. As each new generation overcomes its problems, there accrues the reward of an ever improving standard of living for us all and, hopefully, a rising level of civilized life.

You may become involved in any one of these emerging new career areas on whatever level you choose. All kinds of people will be be needed from a reduced number of laborers and office workers, to an increased number of highly skilled technicians and scientists. Those working in tomorrow's industries on tomorrow's jobs may share psychic satisfactions of knowing that new challenges are being met, new problems solved, and what is probably the greatest satisfaction of all, of knowing that you are playing a part in shaping tomorrow's world.

Appendix A

FUTURISTS: THE FUTURE AND YOU

The World of Tomorrow is being detailed and further expanded by futurists daily. Just since we wrote the first chapter, new developments in creative concepts and insights have occurred. Many people are fascinated by these possibilities of the future. In effect, the futurists are painting the broad scene of the world. They are setting the stage for tomorrow's careers.

Some readers may wish to keep up to date on the latest predictions of the futurists. Others may have found it so fascinating that they are wondering how one becomes a futurist. The following list cites things you can do and activities you can join.

**If You Want To Learn More About Futurism
and the Latest Predictions of the Futurists:**

1. Join the principle futurists' organization: World Future Society, 4916 St. Elmo Avenue, Bethesda, MD 20914 (301) 656-8274. Publications available from W.F.S.:

    The World Future Society Bulletin: a bimonthly journal for professional futurists and others with an interest in futures studies; $18 per year individual; $24 institutional.

    Future Survey: a monthly compilation of abstracts on futures-related topics, $28 individual; $40 institutional.

    Cornish, Edward, and others: *The Study of the Future*; 1977; 320 page paperback, $9.50.

    The Future: A Guide to Information Sources (2nd edition, 1979). 720 page paperback; $25.00

    Feather, Frank, Editor: *Through the 80s Thinking Globally, Acting Locally*; 1980; 430-page paperback, $12.50.

    You may also attend WFS international meetings, held every two years, or be active in a local chapter.

2. Participate in futuristic book and film fairs. An exciting and well-run film fair is offered by Northern Virginia Community College. Check the colleges near you.

3. Take courses, seminars, and workshops on futurism. Check colleges, universities, and adult education facilities in your area.

4. Develop a self-education reading program. Good books to start with are *Future Worlds* by John Gribbin, Plenum Press, 233 Spring Street, New York, N.Y. 10013, 1981. Also Teich, Albert H., Editor: *Technology and Man's Future*, 3rd Edition; St. Martin's Press, Inc., 175 Fifth Avenue, New York, N.Y. 10011; 1981.

5. Subscribe to *What's Next?*, a monthly newsletter of the Congressional Clearinghouse on the Future, 555 House Annex #2, Washington, D.C. 20515. $15.00

6. Be an avid reader of books and articles on futurism. Science fiction can be a good starting point. Speak to your school or community librarian about acquiring the latest books, films, and magazines on futurism.

7. Check the magazine stands for new magazines such as *Next* and *Channels*, or find these in your library's periodical room.

8. Make reference index on cards of all articles which have interested you so you can find them again or recommend them to others.

9. Visit your school, college, private or public library. Ask the librarian about using library sources such as ERIC, and *Books in Print*. Use the Medlar system for medical references.

10. Use industrial information clearinghouses, such as that of Rand and the Hudson Institute. Read their publications. The librarian can help you locate them.

If You Want To Share Your Growing Enthusiasm and Information With Others of Like Interest:

1. Form a human resources network by keeping a card file of knowledgeable people you have met who are interested in future careers and lifestyles. The network might get together for monthly luncheon or dinner meetings.

2. Start a club for futurists where interests and enthusiasms are shared. Get involved in futuristic exercises. Your club can brainstorm for ideas on this. See Appendix B for a list of futurist exercises.

3. Sponsor a book exchange program on futurist subjects such as careers, lifestyles, etc.

If You Wish To Actively Promote Public Awareness of the World of Tomorrow:

1. Schedule futurist speakers for groups to which you belong (professional, trade, religious, union, social, fraternal, etc.).
2. Have a group to which you belong sponsor an essay contest for high school students on "New and Emerging Careers in the World of Tomorrow," or "What Our World Will be Like in the Year 2083." Arrange to have the winning essay appear in the leading newspaper.
3. Investigate local school, junior college, college, and university programs to see what courses in futurism are offered. If none, or very few are offered, take the lead in seeing to it that courses are introduced. Be active in your local school system or board of education.
4. Stimulate your library's interest by donating books, pamphlets, and magazines on futurism. You can take a tax deduction for this as well as help the libraries.
5. Write up some of your ideas and suggestions on future careers and lifestyles and submit them to a local newsletter or newspaper.
6. Write letters to the editor of your local newspaper when items are discussed in the paper that have some baring on futurist careers or lifestyles.
7. At intervals, write letters to your senators and congressman calling their attention to the importance of understanding the future. Express your own interest in this area. Send them pertinent information. Ask them to send you specific information on areas relating to the future such as developments in space, solar energy, etc., including possible legislation that will make a difference in futurist activity.

Springboard Interest Areas In Which You May Wish To Become Involved:

1. For those whose IQs are 130 and above, join Mensa, a group with a strong interest in the future and which has meetings and conferences on this subject. For information write to American Mensa Ltd., 1701 W. 3rd Street, I.R., Brooklyn, N.Y. 11223.
2. Be active in the space program and with those groups who are supporting this thrust. There is no doubt, even though the timing may vary, that the new human frontier is in space.
3. Join a network of people who are interested in expanding their horizons. Your futurists. club may already be a nucleus.

4. Read magazines on creativity or on any other futures related subject of special interest to you. Keep a file of them so they can be retrieved when needed.
5. Attend workshops and seminars on creativity.
6. Take time to think about new ideas or inventions that could make our society more creative and productive, as well as caring and sharing.
7. Invent something that is needed and that can be nationally markketed, or devise a needed service to satisfy a recognized need.
8. Get a job in one of the "newest of the new" industries such as lasers, fiber-optics, computers, robotics, artificial intelligence, solar energy, information handling, electronic banking, etc. Or start a new small business in one of these areas.

As You Become More of An Expert In Futurism, You May:

1. Be available for futuristic talks for various organizations and schools.
2. Conduct seminars, workshops or a course on future careers and lifestyles. These meetings and workshops can be publicized at no cost in many magazines and newsletters.
3. Give short courses on futurism—start as early as grade school.
4. Act as mentor, sponsor, or advisor to others who are seeking futuristic careers.

If You Are Interested In Making Futurism
Your Full-Time Career:

1. You have probably already done a large percentage of things mentioned above. Begin to further expand your network of personal contacts by speaking to leaders and officers or public relations people in some of the industries mentioned above.
2. Speak to people who are deeply involved in futurism such as Herman Kahn, Joseph Coates, Norman Feingold or persons you may have met at a national or international meeting of the World Future Society, or other associations.
3. Re-check your educational needs and qualifications as outlined in the following section.
4. See one of the new breed of career counselors who understand how fast the future is arriving, and some of the changes it will require in human behavior.
5. Armed with brainstorming ideas and concepts, prepare a resume that may open the door for a futuristic position. Check with your professional contacts or with a guidance counselor. Or you

can send your resume to industries, foundations, universities, and other appropriate organizations to see what kind of a response you get. Many futurists who are working in industry are called strategic planners.

6. Read a book on, and talk to your advisors about the art of writing application letters and resumes for futuristic careers.
7. Your advisors may recommend that you write a letter to line up an interview with a working futurist, then present your resume in person during the interview.

A Word About Education and Training

At this time there are no easy answers to the question of how to become a futurist. Futurists are still small in number. Present-day futurists did not train for this field, since it has only recently emerged. They are usually highly educated and experienced in such related fields as space science, psychology, atomic energy, information science, oceanography, or economics. Their work and personal philosophical bents has forced them to think deeply about the shape of things to come.

At the present time, more than 300 colleges and universities offer courses in futures studies, many of them at the graduate level. It is now possible to earn a degree in futures studies, as such, for example, at the University of Houston. A person with this career objective might also work toward a degree in urban studies, education, sociology, or psychology. The emphasis is upon combining methods of science with human understanding developed through behavioral studies, to go on for graduate courses in futures studies.

There will be a growth of people whose main thrust will be as futurists, whether it be in the school, college, university, industry, unions, or a social agency work site. The title "futurist" may refer to a strategic planner, developer, or what have you, but futurists will help guide the destinies of their organizations to further growth and development—or to a premature demise. For some time, the people in this field will probably be those with interdisciplinary education and thrust.

Appendix B

FUTURISTIC EXERCISES

Here are some futuristic exercises designed to be both stimulating and educational.

They are particularly useful with a group of 8 to 10 people. Each group should select a facilitator who helps guide the discussion as well as a recorder who keeps track of what consensus, if any, the group reaches. Suggest to the group that in doing these exercises one's imagination should be expanded. No matter how wild the idea, participants should be willing to present it so that others can test these concepts with their own.

The authors have seen this technique work with groups ranging from children in kindergarten to adults with PhD degrees. Excluding selection time, a minimum of an hour is needed to complete even a few exercises. Here are a few examples of topics to stimulate discussion.

1. The U.S. government has just passed a new law to make for greater efficiency. In all legal and social matters, major purchasers of homes, automobiles, etc., people will now be required to use their social security number rather than their name. How do you feel about this? What effect will it have on our country?

2. Scientists have discovered how to retard aging of cells in humans. People can now live up to 200 years. How will this affect marriage, careers, and the population explosion? What controls or monitoring are necessary? Would you opt to live to 200 years?

3. The U.S. government has decided that the present distribution of jobs and careers in the U.S. will be changed. All positions now occupied by men will be assigned to women after they have taken a one year education and training program. What will the effect be on men and women?

4. You are a well-known scientist who has discovered, after years of research, how to communicate in depth with dolphins. They are

telling you things that will change most people's beliefs all over the world. What do you do?

5. You are a Nobel prize biologist who after years of research finally creates very primitive life in your laboratory. What do you do or not do?

6. Scientists have discovered a new pill with no side effects. If you take it, you will very shortly be brilliant for life. You cannot reverse the process. Will you take the pill?

7. In a future society on earth everyone remains healthy, emotionally and physically, to age 200. Moreover, everyone has an IQ of 200. A few people produce all the food needed. Everyone has all the material possessions he or she wants. What will this society do?

8. Cryologists have now perfected a technique that will allow you to be put to sleep for fifty years and then revived with no change in your physical condition. Will you be willing to try this procedure?

9. The U.S. government has passed a law that everyone has to change his or her career every five years in accordance with each person's abilities, interests, achievements, and personality. How will this affect your life?

10. We can now communicate with all animals. The net effect is that it is now illegal and amoral to eat meat and fish. What changes will take place?

11. You are a married 40-year-old physician in excellent physical shape with in depth knowledge of space. You will be sent to the first moon colony. After five years you are to set up a medical school to train physicians who will take care of the needs of humans in space. What kinds of new specialized educational training will probably be needed? How will you prepare for your own career specialty? You have one year to get ready.

12. An internationally acclaimed chemist discovers how to break down water to perform the same function as gasoline. When, where, and how should she share her discovery?

13. You are assigned the entire responsibility for choosing the first 20 people to colonize a planet similar in climate to earth. You will be the only human inhabitants. None will return for a minimum of ten years. The major criteria is to be the person's career skill plus, of course, excellent health. List the career, age, and sex of the people you will choose and why.

14. The U.S. government has made a law that salaries and total earnings will be reversed. That is the highest level of jobs (such as, a physician, professional atheletes, and corporation presidents) will receive the lowest pay, and lower-level jobs (such as janitor, unskilled

laborer, elevator operator, assembly worker, etc.) will receive the highest salary. What effect will this have on the world of work? How would it effect you?

15. Thousands of men and women with a much higher IQ than ever tested on earth and much more sophisticated equipment even imagined on earth have landed here. Their mission is obviously peace, but their presence is overwhelming. Most people on earth are accepting any of their requests, including education and training. What would you do as a citizen?

16. You work only five hours a day, two days a week. What is your new lifestyle?

17. Science can produce as many duplicate copies of an individual as we wish to have. What are your reactions?

18. You can have your entire body rebuilt, as needed, of artificial parts and life prolonged indefinitely. What will you do?

19. You can choose to live in an experimental satellite circling the earth. Will you volunteer?

20. You live in a domed city under the ocean. What are your reactions?

21. You can communicate using mental telepathy. How do you use this new skill?

22. Retirement is required at age 65, but you live to be 175 years old. What is your reaction?

23. The personalities of your friends are constantly changing because of new personality altering drugs. Will you try them out?

24. Marriage "contracts" are now legal for a limited period of time instead of for life. Do you like this new concept? What will the effect be on marriage?

25. Parents now select the sex of their children in advance. How do you feel about it? What will happen?

26. Private automobiles are outlawed except on certain days. What do you think will happen?

27. You can visit other planets just as you visit other cities today. Where will you go, if at all?

28. You live in a raceless society where all men and women are truly equal—even to the clothes they wear and the houses in which they live. What will happen to society?

29. You are not allowed to own land and have to live in an apartment. What are your reactions?

30. Cures are discovered for all diseases. The only cause of death is very old age. How long do you want to live?

31. Mini-computers are installed in each home for the purpose of

democratically sampling opinions of the people on national issues. Do you like the idea?

32. A machine has been invented that predicts with absolute accuracy the date of a person's death. Will you use it?

33. Before people can marry, they must submit and pass a computer-administered test on 150 correlates of compatibility.

34. Robots take over most of the menial tasks now performed by humans. What will happen to society?

35. People can become invisible. Will you?

36. Man has learned how to bypass human speech and can communicate on higher planes comparable to ESP. Will you communicate in this new mode?

37. Conventional prisons are eliminated in favor of other forms of controlling criminals. (Example: placing electrodes in criminals' brains. If they stray from the territory assigned to them, they experience severe shocks.) Do you think this is a good idea?

38. Electrodes placed within a person's body can serve as identification. The use of credit cards is eliminated. Do you like this method of identification?

39. The great majority of people stop reading and receive their entertainment, news, and other knowledge through media such as television, films, and videotex. What effect will this have on society?

40. A pollution-free electric car is perfected which can reach speeds comparable to those of present cars. It is recharged every 300 miles for half the price of a tank of gasoline. Will you use the new cars?

41. All television sets are programmed to watch you, no matter where you are in your house. Will you own a set?

42. Each female is allowed by law to have only one child during her life-time. Penalties are unusually high. What is the effect on society and you?

43. You are allowed to fill only one small wastebasket with garbage each week or be fined excessively. How will you meet this requirement?

44. You can plug a device into your brain that enables you to feel intense pleasure whenever you like. Will you have it done?

45. You can read other people's minds. What are the positives and negatives?

46. Pills are available that will very quickly give you the skills of any career. Will you take this pill?

47. You can volunteer to join a space colony similar to earth, but

the voyage is so long that there will be no return home. Will you volunteer? Yes or no? Why?

48. Average citizens can volunteer to live under the ocean for one year. Living will be simple but comfortable. Pay and benefits are very high, but there will be no return for a year under any circumstances. Will you go?

49. People with a wide variety of skills are being recruited to make it possible for dead planets to be engineered so that they can support life again. Will you volunteer?

50. A pill has been discovered that makes it possible for the recipients never to need sleep. The change is irreversible. Will you take it?

51. A pill is available that allows you to gradually change your sex within a nine-month period. The method is considered absolutely safe by an eminent physician. Would you change your sex?

52. A compressed artificial food is available at very little cost. It will maintain your health, and you never experience hunger pains. Will you try it?

53. There is solid scientific information from eminent scientists all over the world that there is life after death. What effect will this have on society? What effect will this have on you?

54. A computerized mate selection device is available to the general community. So far the use of this machine has dropped the divorce rate from 75% to 5%. Will you use the machine?

55. An inexpensive device can be implanted in your brain. You can turn it on to dream in color on any topic of your choice. Will you get this dream machine? Yes, no, and why?

56. Synthetic cocaine, heroin, LSD, and qualudes have been made in the laboratory. They are not habit forming or dangerous, and one can derive the usual pleasure associated with these drugs. Will you try them?

57. Planet Zulu has been scanned and studied for over five years in depth by Voyager 298. The U.S. government has decided to send 150 people to settle this planet. The light years distance are too far for the expedition to return. The planet has all kinds of minerals, plants, trees, oceans, and water available, and the gravity is similar to that of the moon. Make up the age, sex, and careers for this expedition, including any screening devices one would use.

58. The U.S. is tremendously interested in the future of our country—particularly the human talent bank. The government is asking for sperm and ova from men and women all over the United States. Will you participate?

59. A meteor, the size of a planet, is headed towards earth at the rate of 25,000 miles per hour, and scientists so far have not been able to divert it from its course or destroy it. It will hit earth in 90 days. Spaceships are available to go to present space colonies but the total people accepted will be at most 100,000. Will you go on to a colony in space or take your chances and stay on earth? Yes, no, and why?

60. A time machine has been available after billions of dollars of research. One can go back in time or in the future for 1,000 years. Will you choose to go back in time or move years ahead? Which, and why?

61. In the event of a nuclear war, only a few citizens can be saved. What are your priorities for those to be saved? Young and physically fit? Skilled specialists? All scientists? Unskilled health professionals? Doctors, dentists, etc.? Old people? Young people? More women than men? Others.

62. A Swedish pharmacutical concern has developed and satisfactorily tested on humans over a period of two decades, an injection that makes children grow to the extent that they weigh from 350 to 450 pounds with appropriate height and appear to be in better health than men of a smaller stature. Would you be willing to give this injection to your son or daughter?

Appendix C

INDEX OF EMERGING CAREER FIELDS
CITED IN THIS BOOK

This index lists the various emerging careers cited in this volume. It is intended as a summary of the career options and a guide to the chapters which cited them. The number after each refers to the chapter where it appears in the "Jobs With A Future" section:

Appendix D

OTHER EMERGING CAREER FIELDS

This appendix lists titles for hundreds of emerging careers that are *not* discussed in this volume. Most of them will be explored in future volumes in this series. For those who wish to learn about these new career opportunities, a review of the technology (such as done in this book) will help provide some immediate clues as to how to best prepare for them.

Agricultural economist
Anesthesiologist assistant
Angio technologist
Animal physiologist
Animal scientist
Applied molecular biologist
Arts manager
Agricultural engineer/technologist
Agricultural communications worker
Audiometric technician
Avian biologist
Battery technician
Behavioral toxicologist
Behavioral pharmacologist
Benefits Analyst
Biochemist
Bioethicist
Biohazard safety specialist
Biomedial engineer
Biomedical X-ray repairperson
Bionic-electronic technician

Biotechnologist
Cable TV auditor
Calibration technician
Cardiovascular perfusionist
Cardiovascular pharmacologist
CAT scanner technician
Cell biologist
Cellular immunologist
Ceramic engineer
Certified alcoholism counselor
Certified financial planner
Certified medication aide
Certified surgical technician
Chemical engineer
Chemist-pharmacologist
Child advocate
Child development associate
Child mental health specialist
Clinical biochemist
Clinical engineer
Clinical pharmacist
Cognitive neurophysiologist
Color consultant

Communications arts technolo-
gist
Communications attorney
Communications consultant
Community ecologist
Community psychologist
Conference planner
Controls/instrumentation spe-
list
Convention manager
Coordinator of government ser-
vices
Corrective therapist
Corporate communications
planner
Cosmetic surgeon
Cost analyst
Counselor, second career plan-
ning
Cryologist
Cryologist technician
Cultural historian
Cytogeneticist
Dance therapist
Dermatobiologist
Developmental biologist
Diagnostic medical sonographer
Diagnostic prescriptive teacher
Economic oceanographer
Educational development officer
Educational media specialist
Electronic engineer
Electronic filer
Electronic mail technician
Electronic hydraulic underseas
specialist
Emergency medical technician
Energy efficiency technician
Energy engineer
Engineering manager
Environmental chemist
Ethicist

Ethnomusicologist
Equal employment investigator
Equipment engineer
Exercise technologist
Family or divorce mediation spe-
cialist
Family therapist
Fiber optic technician
Fire protection engineer
Fire technologist
Floor space manager
Forecasting/public relations spe-
cialist
Forensic scientist
Forest economist
Franchise owner/operator
Garden center manager
Genetic counselor
Genetic counselor coordinator
Genetic engineering technician
Geneticist
Geochemist
Geriatric nurse
Geriatric social worker
Glassblower (laboratory glass-
ware)
Government procurement con-
sultant
Grants application writer
Halfway house manager
Health care administrator
Health lawyer
Health physicist
Health scientist-administrator
Heat transfer specialist
Holographic fiber maintenance
technician
Holographic inspection specialist
Home health aide
House and pet sitter
Horticulture therapy aide
Housing rehabilitation technician

Human factors engineer
Human services worker
Hydroponist
Ice engineer
Immunologist
Indoor air quality scientist
Inhalation therapist
Industrial engineer
Industrial hygiene technician
Industrial laser process technician
Industrial microbiologist
Industrial product design technologist
Information services director
Insect toxicologist
Instrumentation engineer
Invertebrate biochemist
Job developer
Kenesthegiologist
Labor force analyst
Labor development executive
Laser dentist
Laser surgeon
Laser technician
Lead programmer
Leisure counselor
Licensed psychiatric technician
Lodging executive
Loss control engineer
Management and public policy professional
Marina manager
Market development specialist
Marketing communicator
Marketing manager
Massage therapist
Materials utilization technician
Medical anthropologist
Mental health nurse
Microbiologist
Microform technologist
Microsurgeon

Mold engineer
Molecular biologist
Molecular geneticist
Multinational calling officer
Music therapist
Naprapath
Neobiologist
Nuerobiologist
Neuropharmacologist
New frontier director
Nuclear medicine technologist
Nuclear quality assurance inspector
Nursing home counselor
Nurse-midwife
Oceanic hotel manager
Operations statistician
Orthotist/prosthetist
Ornamental horticulturist
Paraprofessional (many fields such as law, social case work, dentistry, medicine, teaching, and veterinary medicine)
Paramedic
Pediatric nurse practioner
Peptide chemist
Personal financial planner
Personal issues manager
Petroleum engineer
Pest management
Physical fitness director
Physical security technician
Physician's assistant
Planetary health officer
Planetary engineer
Planning program manager (government)
Plant biochemist
Plant biologist
Plant biotechnologist
Plant ecologist
Plant geneticist

Plant pathologist
Plant physiologist
Plant therapist
Plastics engineer
Podiatric assistant
Policy analyst
Policy scientist
Pollution botanist
Polygraph examiner
Polymer scientist
Pomotologist
Preservation specialist
Professional electronics file analyst
Professional ethicist
Professional farm manager
Program planner
Psychobiological clinician
Public affairs psychologist
Public historian
Public interest scientist
Public safety communication operator
Publication production technologist
Quality control executive
Race horse breeder
Radiation physicist
Radiologist
Range animal nutritionist
Reconstructive surgeon
Recreation aide
Recreation specialist (theme parks)
Recreation specialist (mentally ill, retarded, or in prisons)
Regulatory specialist
Relocation counselor
Research engineer
Research microbiologist
Research scientist
Research toxicologist

Resource teacher
Retirement counselor
Review coordinator
Risk assessment assistant
Robot salesperson
Sanitarian
Satellite communication engineer
School nurse practioner
School sociologist
Scientific data coordinator
Scientific linguist
Scientific reviewer
Security engineer
Security specialist
Senior marketing research analyst
Service technician
Social director
Sociobiologist
Sociolinguist
Software engineer
Soil physicist
Speech writer
Sports law specialist
Sports psychologist
Spread spectrum specialist
Strategic planner
Stroke rehabilitation nurse
Structured protein chemist
Synthetic materials handler
Systems analyst
Systems architect
Technical planner
Technical service representative
Technical service scientist
Technical service specialist
Technology forecasting specialist
Telecommunications manager
Teratology technician
Test engineer
Thanatologist
Therapeutic recreation technician
Tissue culture technician

Topiatrist
Toxicologist
Toxicology report writer
Transplant coordinator
Ultrasound technologist

Valve engineer
Viral immunologist
Water quality scientist
Wellness consultant

Since the above list was prepared, a number of new fields have come to our attention. They reflect the evolving nature of new careers as many are offshoots of other fields.

Issues manager
Ocean colonist
Acquisitions expert
Spare human organs technician
Energy and life safety systems director
Cancer counselor
Pharmakinetaicist
Reliability engineer
Hotline counselor
Sports medicine expert
Energy banker
Asteroid miner
Tax compliance manager
Surrogate therapist
Bank relationships manager
Computer technology director
Thermal engineer
Biometric security expert
Space botanist
Corporate communications writer
Cable TV auditor
Maintainability engineer
Solar wind technician
Customer service electronic engineer
Avionics analyst
Water expert
International data systems specialist
Biometrician
Management science professional

Financial engineering analyst
Biohazard safety specialist
Imaging engineer
Product planning executive
Tumor immunologist
Arachidonic acid research assistant
Shyness counselor
Microbiological researcher
Hibernation technician
New funds coordinator
Radiation ecologist
Applied biologist
Equestrian science trainer
Technical service manager
Commissioning engineer
Turfgrass research associate
Wildlife ecologist
Quality assurance chemist
Data processing director
Materials manager
Immunodiagnostic sales person
EDP auditor
Temping worker
Technical education sales person
Forecaster
Process development chemist
Design engineer
Biological quality assurance manager
Employee communications associate

Marketing researcher and fore-
caster
Telecommunications analyst
Medical research subject
Electroencephalographer
Population ecologist
New media research analyst

Telecommunications marketing
director
Remote sensing equipment inter-
preter
International systems director
Graphoanalyst

Note: In response to questions from those who reviewed the early drafts of the book, it might be well to add a few words on sources used to discover emerging occupations.

These lists were compiled from a wide variety of recent daily, weekly, and monthly newspapers, newsletters and magazines, published by trade and professional associations and publishers. Some represent different names assigned to the same or very similar jobs. Some re-name traditional careers which have been radically changed in nature. Others reflect attempts to name new and different functional, break-downs of areas of responsibility, caused by computerization which has enabled individual workers to handle broader areas. Many are names for wholly new occupations which never existed before. Among these appear many new, very narrow, highly technical specialties.

Taken all together these new careers reflect the transition taking place in the work place as we move into the age of information. For some it is unsettling. Others see it as a widening of opportunities, and are exhilarated by the many challenges.

Order/Interest Form

To: Garrett Park Press
     Garrett Park, Maryland 20896

Please send _____ copies of *Emerging Careers: New Occupations for the Year 2000 and Beyond.*

☐ Check for $10.95 per copy enclosed
☐ Bill our organization for $11.95 per copy

(Note: Orders from individuals should be prepaid)

Ship to: Bill to (if different):

_____   _____

_____   _____

_____   _____

I have already read the first volume in this series. Please notify me when subsequent volumes in the *Emerging Careers* series become available:

Name: _____

Title: _____

Organization: _____

Address: _____

Order/Interest Form

To: Garrett Park Press
     Garrett Park, Maryland 20896

Please send _____ copies of *Emerging Careers: New Occupations for the Year 2000 and Beyond.*

☐ Check for $10.95 per copy enclosed
☐ Bill our organization for $11.95 per copy

(Note: Orders from individuals should be prepaid)

Ship to: Bill to (if different):

_____   _____

_____   _____

_____   _____

I have already read the first volume in this series. Please notify me when subsequent volumes in the *Emerging Careers* series become available:

Name: _____

Title: _____

Organization: _____

Address: _____

Order/Interest Form

To: Garrett Park Press
     Garrett Park, Maryland 20896

Please send _____ copies of *Emerging Careers: New Occupations for the Year 2000 and Beyond.*

☐ Check for $10.95 per copy enclosed
☐ Bill our organization for $11.95 per copy
          (Note: Orders from individuals should be prepaid)

Ship to: Bill to (if different):

_____   _____

_____   _____

_____   _____

I have already read the first volume in this series. Please notify me when subsequent volumes in the *Emerging Careers* series become available:

     Name: _____

     Title: _____

     Organization: _____

     Address: _____

- -

Order/Interest Form

To: Garrett Park Press
     Garrett Park, Maryland 20896

Please send _____ copies of *Emerging Careers: New Occupations for the Year 2000 and Beyond.*

☐ Check for $10.95 per copy enclosed
☐ Bill our organization for $11.95 per copy
          (Note: Orders from individuals should be prepaid)

Ship to: Bill to (if different):

_____   _____

_____   _____

_____   _____

I have already read the first volume in this series. Please notify me when subsequent volumes in the *Emerging Careers* series become available:

     Name: _____

     Title: _____

     Organization: _____

     Address: _____